THE BIG BOOK OF AMAZING ACTIVITIES

crossword

Buster Books

D1354422

This awesome activity book is bursting with activities to choose from. From colouring and doodling to dot to dots, paper craft and brain-teaser puzzles, it's time to pick an activity and have some fun! You can check all your answers to the puzzles at the back of the book.

What are you waiting for?

First published in Great Britain in 2014 by Buster Books,
an imprint of Michael O'Mara Books Limited,
9 Lion Yard, Tremadoc Road, London SW4 7NQ

Compilation copyright © Buster Books 2014
Illustrations and layouts © Buster Books
2005, 2006, 2008, 2009, 2011, 2012, 2013, 2014
Wordsearch and crossword puzzles and solutions © Gareth Moore 2011
Sudoku puzzles and solutions copyright © Alastair Chisholm 2005
The right of Alastair Chisholm to be identified as the author of the puzzles
taken from *The Kids' Book of Sudoku Book 1*, has been asserted in accordance
with sections 77 and 78 of the Copyright Designs and Patents Act 1988.

Designed by Jack Clucas
Edited by Hannah Cohen
Illustrations by Hannah Davies, Tony Payne, Andrew Pinder,
Emily Golden Twomey and Joanna Webster
Paper craft by Tony Payne
Wordsearch and crossword puzzles and solutions by Dr Gareth Moore
Puzzles designed and typeset by Gareth Moore www.drgarethmoore.com
Sudoku puzzles and solutions by Alastair Chisholm
Dominos, number searches, Tai-Chi towers and cosmic connectors
puzzles and solutions by Ellen Nowak

This book contains material previously published in *The Kids' Book of
Crosswords, The Kids' Book of Wordsearches, The Kids' Book Of Holiday Puzzles,
Dot To Dot, Buster's Brilliant Dot To Dot, Colour By Numbers, Buster's Brilliant Colour
By Numbers, The Kids' Book of Sudoku Book 1, The Creative Colouring Book,
The Girls' Fabulous Colouring Book, The Girls' Glorious Colouring Book,
The Boys' Doodle Book, The Girls' Doodle Book, Things To
Make and Doodle* and *The Kids' Book of Number Puzzles.*

With additional material adapted from www.shutterstock.com

A CIP catalogue record for this book is available from the British Library.

ISBN: 978-1-78055-293-4
2 4 6 8 10 9 7 5 3

This book was printed in January 2015 by Leo Paper Products Ltd, Heshan Astros Printing Limited,
Xuantan Temple Industrial Zone, Gulao Town, Heshan City, Guangdong Province, China.

 www.busterbooks.co.uk Buster Children's Books 🐦 @BusterBooks

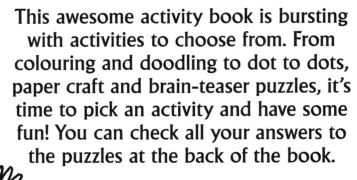

1 = purple   2 = red   3 = blue

4 = yellow   5 = green   6 = pink   7 = orange

Put on a puppet show.

DOODLING

Build the world's biggest snowman.

Colour by numbers grid:

1	1	2	1	1	1	1	1	1	1	1	1	1	2	1	1
1	1	2	2	2	2	1	1	1	1	2	2	2	2	1	1
1	1	1	1	1	2	2	2	2	2	2	1	1	1	1	1
3	3	3	1	1	1	1	2	2	1	1	1	1	3	3	3
3	3	3	3	3	1	1	5	5	1	1	3	3	3	3	3
4	4	4	4	3	3	1	6	6	1	3	3	4	4	4	4
4	4	5	5	5	3	1	7	7	1	3	5	5	5	4	4
1	4	2	2	2	3	3	6	6	3	3	2	2	2	4	1
1	4	2	7	2	4	4	7	7	4	4	2	7	2	4	1
1	4	2	2	2	2	4	6	6	4	2	2	2	2	4	1
1	1	5	5	5	4	4	7	7	4	4	5	5	5	1	1
1	1	1	4	4	4	4	6	6	4	4	4	4	1	1	1
1	1	1	1	1	3	3	7	7	3	3	1	1	1	1	1
1	1	1	3	3	3	3	6	6	3	3	3	3	1	1	1
1	1	3	3	4	4	4	7	7	4	4	4	3	3	1	1
3	3	3	4	4	4	4	6	6	4	4	4	4	3	3	3
4	4	2	2	2	2	4	7	7	4	2	2	2	2	4	4
4	4	2	7	2	4	1	6	6	1	4	2	7	2	4	4
1	4	2	5	2	1	1	7	7	1	1	2	5	2	4	1
1	1	2	2	2	1	1	6	6	1	1	2	2	2	1	1
1	1	1	4	4	1	1	1	1	1	1	4	4	1	1	1
1	1	1	1	4	1	1	1	1	1	1	4	1	1	1	1

1 = green   2 = purple   3 = red   4 = pink   5 = blue   6 = brown   7= yellow

1 = blue   2 = green   3 = red   4 = pink   5 = orange   6 = yellow   7 = brown

COLOURING

Draw a weird alien here ...

... and draw the planet that it lives on here.

1 = red   2 = orange   3 = yellow   4 = pink

5 = purple   6 = green   7 = brown   8 = blue

What has he caught?

Sweet dreams ...

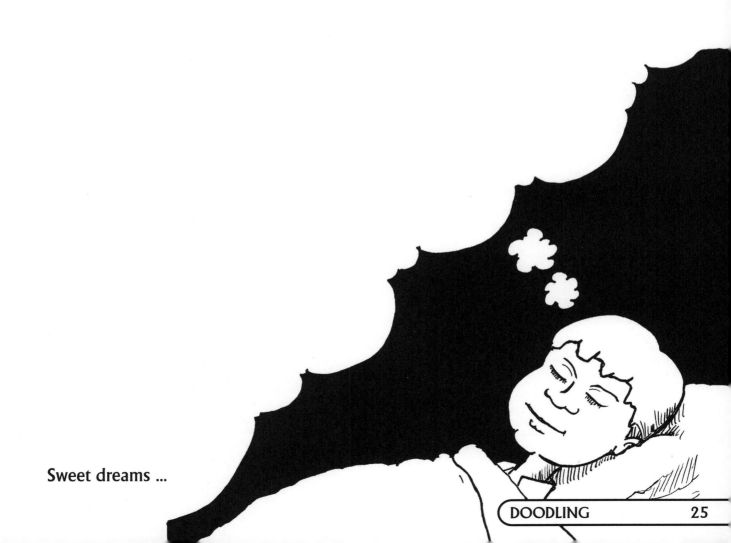

CROSSWORDS

The crosswords in this section will test your word power. The rules are very simple: just find the solution word described by each numbered across or down clue and then write it into the corresponding squares in the grid. Sometimes, you will be able to think of more than one solution to a clue. When this happens, wait until you solve some of the words that cross over that one in the grid, then use these to help you choose the correct solution.

Each clue has a number in brackets at the end, like this: (4). This shows you how many letters are in the word you are trying to guess and matches the number of empty squares in the grid. Occasionally you might see two numbers, like this: (3, 3). This means there are two words to place, each of the given length, such as 'The End'. Don't leave a space between the words in the grid, though – write one letter in each square. If you see a ';' in a clue, it means the clue is made up of different parts which will help you guess the solution. For example, the clue: 'Opposite of front; rear of your body (4)' provides two clues for 'back'.

The crosswords get harder as you work through the section. If you get completely stuck, don't panic – all of the answers are in the back of the book.

Puzzle: 1

Across
1 Large, edible fish with pink flesh (6)
4 Useful (7)
6 Leafy, green vegetable that Popeye eats (7)
8 Hang or swing loosely (6)

Down
1 Clean the floor with a broom (5)
2 Part of the body; one circuit of a track (3)
3 A score of nothing in a football match (3)
5 Parent's brother (5)
6 Not happy (3)
7 Pester or repeatedly complain to someone (3)

Puzzle: 2

Across
1 Push something down firmly (5)
4 Something a child plays with (3)
5 Turns over and over (5)
6 Add some numbers (3,2)
7 A knight's title, ___ Galahad, for example (3)
8 Deep spoon with long handle, often used to serve soup (5)

Down
1 Ancient Egyptian monument (7)
2 Shadow of the Earth on the moon (7)
3 Female sibling (6)
4 Glittery material used to decorate Christmas trees (6)

Puzzle: 3

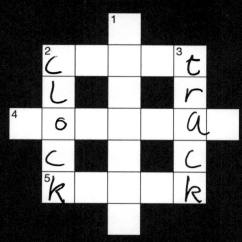

Across
2 Plan or diagram; a pie or bar _____ (5)
4 Diary to write thoughts in (7)
5 Tap on a door (5)

Down
1 Another word for a soldier or fighter (7)
2 Something that tells the time (5)
3 Something trains run on (5)

Puzzle: 4

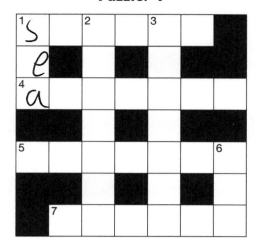

Across
1 Trip to see wild animals in their natural homes (6)
4 Leave behind (7)
5 A difficult task; something that worries you (7)
7 Someone who shoots bows and arrows (6)

Down
1 Large expanse of water between countries (3)
2 Taste (7)
3 Name of one of Santa's reindeers (7)
6 Spoil something (3)

Puzzle: 5

Across
2 Superhero's cloak (4)
4 Person who does something brave (4)
5 An army officer of high rank (5)
6 For example: kitchen, lounge or hall (4)
7 Lazy (4)

Down
1 Mythical creature with a woman's body and a fish's tail (7)
2 Perform a magic trick (7)
3 Ancient Egyptian king (7)

Puzzle: 6

Across
1 Small, dark red fruit on a stalk with a stone in the centre (6)
4 Long, stringy food served with many Oriental meals (7)
6 Take your clothes off (7)

Down
1 Might go on a Queen's head (5)
2 The point where something stops (3)
3 Word for agreeing (3)
5 Stand used by artist to hold a canvas while painting (5)
6 Utilise something (3)
7 Male sheep (3)

Puzzle: 7

Across
1 Short version of 'Christmas' (4)
4 For example: drawings, paintings, sculptures and music (3)
6 Grand house (7)
7 Wheel with teeth used in mechanisms (3)
8 Reflection of sound (4)

Down
2 Picture made with small coloured tiles (6)
3 Long tube of minced meat, often served with mash (7)
5 Narrow box for animals to eat from (6)

Puzzle: 8

Across
2 Cereal plant used to make flour (5)
4 Male sibling (7)
5 Medium-sized sailing boat (5)

Down
1 Green, leafy salad vegetable (7)
2 Anxiety; something you are concerned about (5)
3 Something you enjoy; a reward (5)

Puzzle: 9

Across
4 Young frog without legs (7)
5 Tool used to tighten bolts (7)
6 Hide (7))

Down
1 Spear used to catch whales (7)
2 Dark green, leafy vegetable (7)
3 Against the law (7)

Puzzle: 10

Across
2 Home of Winnie the Pooh, Hundred ____ Wood (4)
4 Something you eat (4)
5 Big; sizeable (5)
6 Something a plant grows from (4)
7 Glass part of spectacles (4)

Down
1 Picture made by sticking together scraps of paper (7)
2 Details of where someone lives (7)
3 Official at a football match (7)

Puzzle: 11

Across
1 Large, soft feather (5)
4 Solemn promise (3)
6 Living; existing (5)
7 Vegetable that makes you cry (5)
8 Part of the body used for listening (3)
9 Time of day you might see the moon (5)

Down
1 The Black Death, for example (6)
2 Mythical one-horned animal (7)
3 Part of the day just before bedtime (7)
5 Edible nut with a wrinkly surface (6)

Puzzle: 12

Across
1 Small animals or insects that carry disease or are harmful to crops (6)
4 Silky material (5)
6 Small juicy fruit containing seeds in its flesh (5)
8 Attractive; nice to look at (6)

Down
1 Stopping at en route, as in 'The train went from London to Southampton _ _ _ Basingstoke' (3)
2 Large country house with grounds (5)
3 Unpleasant; horrible (5)
4 Clever; the opposite of blunt (5)
5 Furniture with legs and a flat top (5)
7 Thin beam of sunlight (3)

Puzzle: 13

Across
1 Coldest season of the year (6)
4 Error (7)
6 Waterproof boots (7)
8 A shape or sign that means something (6)

Down
1 Put words on paper (5)
2 The opposite of something, as in 'I will do this but _ _ _ that' (3)
3 Cereal used in bread and biscuits; a famous book called 'The Catcher in the _ _ _' (3)
5 Sit down on your knees (5)
6 Used to be (3)
7 Overhead shot in tennis (3)

Puzzle: 14

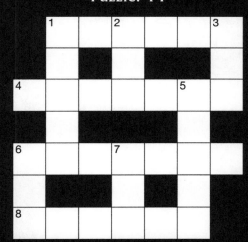

Across
1 Linked to the universe (6)
4 Write a piece of music (7)
6 Strange; rare (7)
8 A common citrus fruit (6)

Down
1 Circus performer with bright red nose (5)
2 Drink in small quantities (3)
3 Line of text used to prompt an actor (3)
5 A fright (5)
6 Unidentified flying object (abbreviation) (1,1,1)
7 Our closest star (3)

Puzzle: 15

Across
1 Fading light in the early evening (4)
3 What you might call a male teacher (3)
5 Spoon used for serving soft food, such as ice cream (5)
6 Sharp cutting tool (5)
7 Utter a word or sentence (3)
8 Not pleasant to look at (4)

Down
1 A heavy disk thrown during athletic events (6)
2 Ghostly; creepy (6)
3 Coiled spiral of metal wire, often found in a mattress (6)
4 Cure for an illness (6)

Puzzle: 16

Across
1 Noise made by a duck (5)
5 Person being treated by a doctor (7)
6 Toy with two wheels, which yoa foot (7)
7 Small garden ornament with beard and pointed hat (5)

Down
2 Standard outfit everyone at the same place wears (7)
3 Decide not to do something; an on-screen button to say 'no' to an option (6)
4 Small type of hawk (6)

Puzzle: 17

Across
3 Used for taking photographs (6)
4 In support of (3)
5 Untidy; dirty (5)
7 Male pig (3)
8 Voucher (6)

Down
1 Female horse (4)
2 Wax colouring item (6)
3 Ordinary; usual (6)
6 Outer covering for your foot (4)

Puzzle: 18

Across
2 Food selected to help someone become healthier (4)
4 String used to tie up a shoe (4)
5 Fourth month (5)
6 Loose earth (4)
7 Grated peel of a lemon or orange (4)

Down
1 Singing along and following words on a screen (7)
2 Unfreeze (7)
3 To shout or speak suddenly (7)

Puzzle: 19

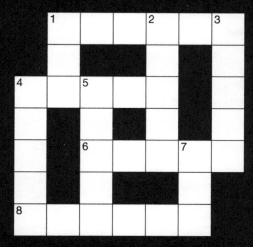

Across
1 Prehistoric animal remains found in rock (6)
4 Precious stone (5)
6 Newly made (5)
8 Sadness (6)

Down
1 Payment; charge (3)
2 Work out a solution (5)
3 Meal at midday (5)
4 Trousers made of denim (5)
5 Thin biscuit (5)
7 Noticed something, as in 'I ___ it happen' (3)

Puzzle: 20

Across
1 Instrument often pictured being played by angels (4)
4 Tear something, such as a piece of paper (3)
6 Male who delivers letters (7)
7 Container for storing rubbish (3)
8 Be brave enough to do something (4)

Down
2 Soak up some liquid (6)
3 Imagine something is real (7)
5 Words you address to God (6)

Puzzle: 21

Across
4 Machine for carrying people or goods (7)
5 Warm up your muscles before exercise (7)
6 Thin, crispy biscuit (7)

Down
1 The characters that make up the alphabet (7)
2 Absolute quiet (7)
3 Slow-moving mass of ice found on land (7)

Puzzle: 22

Across
3 People who catch criminals (6)
4 Female parent (3)
5 A time without war (5)
7 Not strict (3)
8 A light gas used to fill floating balloons (6)

Down
1 Tall, rounded roof (4)
2 Loud, shrill cry (6)
3 Doll controlled by hand, sometimes with strings (6)
6 A group where people enjoy the same hobby; black playing card (4)

Puzzle: 23

Across
1 Back bones (5)
5 Noise that accompanies lightning (7)
6 Thick, sticky liquid made from sugar (7)
7 Animal kept for wool and meat (5)

Down
2 Food made on Shrove Tuesday (7)
3 Thin piece of metal used for sewing (6)
4 Christian building of worship (6)

Puzzle: 24

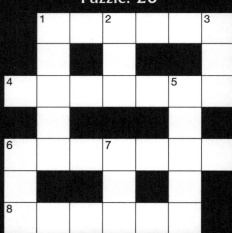

Across
2 Huge person in fairy tales (5)
4 Difficult; complicated (7)
5 Walk like a soldier (5)

Down
1 Blood-sucking monster (7)
2 Someone who looks after horses (5)
3 What you bite your food with (5)

Puzzle: 25

Across
1 A rich, moist cake, often topped with cherries (6)
4 Someone who educates you (7)
5 Woman in a play (7)
7 Someone you like and know (6)

Down
1 Instinctive thought: a _ _ _ feeling (3)
2 Vehicle used on farms (7)
3 A sports player (7)
6 Unhappy (3)

Puzzle: 26

Across
1 Well known (6)
4 Place to catch a train (7)
6 Speak secretively (7)
8 Fantasy fire-breathing beast (6)

Down
1 Go and bring (5)
2 Came across someone (3)
3 Male child (3)
5 Large sea (5)
6 Marry someone (3)
7 To drop or sink to a lower level (3)

Puzzle: 27

Across
2 Cow's meat (4)
4 Group two things together (4)
5 Complete; absolute (5)
6 Often goes with pepper (4)
7 Traditional story about gods and heroes (4)

Down
1 First month of the year (7)
2 From Great Britain (7)
3 A green precious stone (7)

Puzzle: 28

Across
1 Male parent (6)
4 White granules sometimes added to sweeten tea or coffee (5)
6 Each one; all of something (5)
8 Opening in a wall, usually filled with glass (6)

Down
1 Short for 'influenza' (3)
2 For example, Black Beauty (5)
3 To answer someone (5)
4 Long, narrow tube for drinking (5)
5 Colour for 'go' (5)
7 Use oars to move a boat (3)

Puzzle: 29

Across
2 Rub out (5)
4 Soldiers on horses (7)
5 Rope for leading a dog (5)

Down
1 Holiday vehicle for camping (7)
2 Electronic mail (5)
3 Our planet (5)

Puzzle: 30

Across
4 This evening (7)
5 Gentle rain (7)
6 Red, orange, yellow, green, blue, indigo and violet (7)

Down
1 Small carpet for wiping your feet on (7)
2 Making lots of small bubbles (7)
3 Opposite of deep (7)

Puzzle: 31

Across
2 Notice board; in astrology, which star ____ are you? (4)
4 A walking track (4)
5 The overall amount (5)
6 Organ used for breathing (4)
7 Very tall plant with branches and leaves (4)

Down
1 Big black leopard (7)
2 Vehicle travelling back and forth (7)
3 A wreath of flowers worn around the neck or hung up (7)

Puzzle: 32

Across
1 On time; without delay (6)
4 Opposite of light (5)
6 Before all the others (5)
8 Primary painting colour (6)

Down
1 Mince ___, eaten at Christmas (3)
2 Person in charge of a town who wears a gold chain (5)
3 Grilled bread (5)
4 Cheery; contented (5)
5 Very bad (5)
7 Female pig (3)

Puzzle: 33

Across
3 Soft floor covering (6)
4 Reddish, dog-like animal (3)
5 Small fairy (5)
7 Opposite of wet (3)
8 Something you must keep to yourself (6)

Down
1 A cab (4)
2 Large area of dry land, often covered in sand (6)
3 Red-brown metal used in wires (6)
6 Thought (4)

Puzzle: 34

Across
1 Instructions for cooking food (6)
4 Greet on arrival (7)
5 Unusual; different (7)
7 Long-stemmed, crunchy green vegetable, often eaten raw (6)

Down
1 Not cooked (3)
2 School for continuing education (7)
3 Say that you will definitely do something (7)
6 Produce an egg, if you're a hen (3)

Puzzle: 35

Across
1 To handle a situation (4)
3 Said to someone when you leave them (3)
5 Woolly animal, like a smaller camel without a hump (5)
6 Joint of your arm (5)
7 For example: brazil, hazel, almond (3)
8 Pull something heavy (4)

Down
1 Pillar, often found in Greek and Roman ruins (6)
2 For example: Earth, Jupiter or Mars (6)
3 Hairdresser for men (6)
4 Small crawling insect with pincers (6)

Puzzle: 36

Across
1 Not very happy (5)
5 Someone who visits places abroad (7)
6 Spectacles (7)
7 The measurement between two lines that meet at a point (5)

Down
2 Light umbrella used in the sunshine (7)
3 Christian festival during spring (6)
4 Powder inside a flower (6)

Puzzle: 37

Across
3 About the sea; name for a soldier serving on board a ship (6)
4 Object used to cool yourself (3)
5 Raised platform for theatre shows (5)
7 Covered in ice (3)
8 The opposite of arrive (6)

Down
1 Feel you would like something, as in 'I ____ this' (4)
2 Small creature with six legs (6)
3 Man in charge (6)
6 Female child (4)

Puzzle: 38

Across
2 Circular device found on cars (5)
4 Something old and valuable (7)
5 Time when you are young; type of club for young people (5)

Down
1 Not funny (7)
2 Blustery, as in 'this is _____ weather' (5)
3 Giggle (5)

Puzzle: 39

Across
1 From France (6)
4 Glasses worn for swimming (7)
6 Something that is difficult to solve (7)
8 Not anyone (6)

Down
1 What you walk on (5)
2 Object laid by birds, fish, reptiles and insects (3)
3 Owns (3)
5 A person who is against you (5)
6 Metal fastening (3)
7 Shout disapproval (3)

Puzzle: 40

Across
1 Small mark (4)
4 Found at the top of the thigh; the fruit of a rose (3)
6 Remove clothing (7)
7 Slice with a knife (3)
8 Yellow part of an egg (4)

Down
2 Meal packed to eat outside, such as in the park (6)
3 Needing a drink (7)
5 Chalk crayon (6)

Puzzle: 41

Across
1 Jar for holding flowers (4)
3 Flying night-time animal (3)
5 Delicate pottery (5)
6 Pale (5)
7 In the middle of (3)
8 Not costing anything (4)

Down
1 _ _ _ _ _ _ cleaner, used for hoovering (6)
2 Protection carried by a soldier (6)
3 Nocturnal black and white animal (6)
4 Sea animal with a hard shell on its back (6)

Puzzle: 42

Across
1 The opposite of full (5)
5 A gift from someone (7)
6 Belonging to the same family (7)
7 A room used for writing and reading (5)

Down
2 Hot-tasting yellow food paste, often added to ham (7)
3 Glittery material used to decorate Christmas trees (6)
4 Religious leader (6)

Puzzle: 43

Across
2 Cut shorter (4)
4 Market (4)
5 Vegetable that makes you cry; a crisp flavour, 'cheese and _____' (5)
6 The opposite direction to West (4)
7 Fast, graceful animal with antlers (4)

Down
1 Light-weight waterproof coat (7)
2 Sports shoe with rubber sole (7)
3 Sickness (7)

Puzzle: 44

Across
1 Plant on which grapes grow (4)
4 To be able; 'I ___ do this' (3)
6 Large bird that eats flesh from dead animals (7)
7 Opposite of 'no' (3)
8 Shout loudly (4)

Down
2 Harm done to someone (6)
3 Great joy; intense emotion (7)
5 Everyday; regular (6)

Puzzle: 45

Across
2 Board game with kings, queens and pawns (5)
4 Damage; ruin something (7)
5 Doctor's assistant (5)

Down
1 One hundred years (7)
2 Tidy up; neaten (5)
3 A small piece of rock (5)

Puzzle: 46

Across
1 Large bird that gobbles (6)
4 Large bird with pouch in beak for holding fish (7)
5 Ancient Egyptian king (7)
7 Envelope contents (6)

Down
1 Hit something gently (3)
2 Let go of something (7)
3 Put a magic spell on someone; delight someone (7)
6 Belonging to the woman or girl (3)

Puzzle: 47

Across
2 Travel through water using your hands and feet (4)
4 A long way down, especially under water (4)
5 For example: sight, hearing, touch, taste or smell (5)
6 Black substance mined and used for fuel (4)
7 Scratch (4)

Down
1 Pudding (7)
2 Leafy, dark green vegetable (7)
3 Unlawful; forbidden (7)

Puzzle: 48

Across
1 Secret plan to do something bad (4)
4 An obligation to repay something (3)
6 Girl's bag for carrying a purse (7)
7 When something is expected to arrive it is '___'; need to be paid (3)
8 Small loaf of bread (4)

Down
2 Small, four-legged reptile with a long tail (6)
3 Young child who has started to walk (7)
5 The white surface of teeth (6)

Puzzle: 49

Across
2 Bad weather with thunder and lightning (5)
4 Brave; courageous (7)
5 Hard black wood, sometimes used for piano keys (5)

Down
1 Line where the sky meets the Earth (7)
2 Outline of something; a square, circle and triangle are all types of _ _ _ _ _ (5)
3 Coins or notes used to buy things (5)

Puzzle: 50

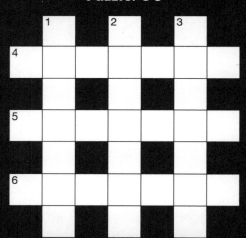

Across
4 Official at a football match (7)
5 Badly behaved (7)
6 Young goose (7)

Down
1 Shape with six sides (7)
2 Common white or grey seabird (7)
3 Fate (7)

Puzzle: 51

Across
2 Thin layer covering a surface (4)
4 Mix with a spoon (4)
5 Do very well at something (5)
6 The bottom of your ear (4)
7 Hard clothing you put on your foot (4)

Down
1 Warm up your muscles before exercise (7)
2 Small, brown mark on skin (7)
3 Bedtime song for babies (7)

Puzzle: 52

Across
1 On a ship (6)
4 Entertain someone (5)
6 Book for keeping day-by-day notes of what someone does (5)
8 Scottish cloth with coloured patterns (6)

Down
1 A goal or target (3)
2 Where sports events take place (5)
3 Place where milk is processed (5)
4 No longer a child (5)
5 Beneath; below (5)
7 Move quickly on foot (3)

Puzzle: 53

Across
1 Area around the North Pole (6)
4 Shopkeeper selling flowers (7)
6 Clothing worn in bed (7)
8 Planted ground around a house (6)

Down
1 Narrow street or passage (5)
2 Motor vehicle (3)
3 Feline animal (3)
5 A mark on clothes (5)
6 Farm animal with a snout and a curly tail (3)
7 If you cut yourself, you may need first ___ (3)

Puzzle: 54

Across
1 Talk; say something (5)
4 Large expanse of water between countries (3)
5 Liquid put on walls to decorate (5)
6 Foolish person (5)
7 Say something that isn't true (3)
8 Large bird of prey (5)

Down
1 Young tree (7)
2 Biblical letter (7)
3 Device for boiling water (6)
4 Light a match (6)

Puzzle: 55

Across
1 Eleventh month (8)
5 Substance used for making crayons and candles (3)
6 Juicy tropical fruit (5)
8 Police officer (9)
10 Pinkish-yellow juicy fruit with furry skin (5)
13 Bite sharply, like a dog might do (3)
15 Heavy fall of rain (8)

Down
1 At this time (3)
2 Female fox (5)
3 Sound made by a sheep (3)
4 Old piece of cloth (3)
6 Small stick struck to create a flame (5)
7 A single item (3)
8 Soft, flat hat (3)
9 Long-necked musical instrument with strings to pluck (5)
11 A Muslim festival (3)
12 Farmyard animal that produces milk (3)
14 For each, as in 'one ___ person' (3)

Puzzle: 56

Across
4 Warning sound (5)
6 Piece of writing with rhyming lines (4)
7 Gang or crowd who are hard to control (3)
9 Wicked person, especially in a story (7)
10 Playing card '1' (3)
12 Glass part of a telescope or spectacles (4)
13 Copy a picture by drawing over it on thin paper (5)

Down
1 Bet money on something (6)
2 Between your shoulder and your hand (3)
3 Criminal in prison (7)
5 First part of the day (7)
8 Large, wooden hammer (6)
11 Do something wrongly (3)

Puzzle: 57

Across
1 Get pleasure from (5)
3 The cover over a building (4)
5 Hover in the air (5)
8 Someone who travels in a spaceship (9)
9 Sharp point growing on a rose stem (5)
11 Noise made by a clock (4)
12 Opposite of loud (5)

Down
1 Small mischievous fairy (3)
2 Whirlwind (7)
4 Something that is true (4)
6 Large bird that can run fast but can't fly (7)
7 Edible freshwater fish (5)
8 Parent's sister (4)
10 Something used to catch fish with (3)

Puzzle: 58

Across
1 What comes out when you turn the tap on (5)
4 Weapon for shooting arrows (3)
6 High-ranking teacher (9)
7 Plant used for food, some of which are also called 'greens' (9)
10 A joke based on multiple meanings of words (3)
11 Someone who flies an aeroplane (5)

Down
1 Cry (4)
2 Sledge for sliding downhill (8)
3 Competition to arrive first (4)
4 Popular American ball game similar to Rounders (8)
5 Period of fighting between armies (3)
7 Very important person (abbreviation) (1,1,1)
8 Short journey (4)
9 Change (4)

Puzzle: 59

Across
1 Word used to introduce a contrasting viewpoint (3)
3 Real or correct (4)
5 The pink flesh around your teeth (3)
6 Small mug for tea (3)
8 Real-life picture (5)
9 The length of time that a person has been alive (3)
10 Short sleep (3)
11 Hard; not easy to bend (5)
13 Warm (3)
15 Climbing evergreen plant, often grows up buildings (3)
17 Story (4)
18 The cat sat on the ___ (3)

Down
1 Creepy-crawly (3)
2 Violent storm (7)
3 Group of three people (4)
4 Large, Australian, flightless bird (3)
6 Agree with (7)
7 Small seed found in fruit (3)
9 The blackened remains of a fire (3)
12 A small island (4)
14 Not in (3)
16 So far; up until now (3)

Puzzle: 60

Across
1 Last month of the year (8)
5 Loud noise (3)
6 Incorrect (5)
8 Exactly the same (9)
10 Soil; ground (5)
13 Having lived for a long time (3)
15 Someone who looks after sheep (8)

Down
1 Disc with a film or TV show on it (abbreviation) (1,1,1)
2 Small boat with a paddle (5)
3 A metal pole (3)
4 Did go for a run (3)
6 Look at a television set (5)
7 Substance for styling hair (3)
8 Frozen water (3)
9 Shut something (5)
11 A donkey (3)
12 Definite article; a particular item, as in 'I want ___ one over there' (3)
14 Past tense of 'do', as in 'what I ___ yesterday' (3)

Puzzle: 61

Across
1 Thin paper used for blowing your nose (6)
4 Thick black liquid used for surfacing roads (3)
5 Mark left after an injury has healed (4)
7 Sorrow; misfortune (3)
10 Large country house, especially in Roman times (5)
11 Make an offer in an auction (3)
13 Join two things together (4)
16 The edge of a hole; part of your mouth (3)
17 Bicycle for two people (6)

Down
1 Have a go at an activity (3)
2 Urgent call for help (abbreviation) (1,1,1)
3 Small job; chore (6)
4 An even number just less than three (3)
6 Sideways-walking shellfish with pincers and legs (4)
7 Case to carry money in (6)
8 Whole numbers are either ____ or odd (4)
9 Airborne insect (3)
12 Mischievous pixie (3)
14 Tease; a child (3)
15 Tall tree with broad leaves (3)

Puzzle: 62

Across
1 Opposite of white (5)
3 Measurement used in the USA as a small measure of length (4)
5 Come into flower (5)
8 Washing powder (9)
9 Home for a rabbit (5)
11 Part of your body used for walking on (4)
12 Land for growing crops (5)

Down
1 Float gently up and down in water (3)
2 Really old (7)
4 Clue (4)
6 Halloween month (7)
7 Third month (5)
8 Unable to hear (4)
10 Did own (3)

Puzzle: 63

Across
1 Foolish (5)
4 Place where adults buy drinks (3)
6 Say sorry (9)
7 Type of music composed by Mozart (9)
10 Fasten; ___ your shoelaces (3)
11 Unpleasant; horrible (5)

Down
1 Long, soft seat for more than one person (4)
2 Flavoured fruit drink (8)
3 Round toy that goes up and down on a string (2-2)
4 Daughter of a king and queen (8)
5 Pollinating insect (3)
7 Baby's bed (3)
8 Graceful white water bird (4)
9 Woman (4)

Puzzle: 64

Across
1 Great happiness (3)
3 Choose something (3)
5 What we breathe (3)
7 TV company, 'British Broadcasting Corporation' (abbreviation) (1,1,1)
8 Avoid (5)
10 Colourfully-winged insect (9)
13 Problem with a computer program (5)
16 You must ___ and drink to stay alive (3)
18 Belonging to us (3)
19 Father (3)
20 The person I am talking to (3)

Down
1 Work done for money (3)
2 Medium-sized sailing boat (5)
3 A rock with metal in it (3)
4 Hot, brewed drink (3)
6 To a great amount, as in 'she was ____ happy' (4)
9 Video cassette recorder (abbreviation) (1,1,1)
10 Meat of a cow (4)
11 Also; as well (3)
12 Full of flames (5)
14 Discard something unwanted (3)
15 A long thin stick, such as one used for fishing (3)
17 Abbreviation for the day after Wednesday (3)

Puzzle: 65

Across
4 Common; ordinary (5)
6 A light-brown colour (4)
7 Ask people in the street to give you money (3)
9 The gathering of crops (7)
10 Wheel with teeth used in mechanisms (3)
12 Large farm building used for storage (4)
13 Book containing a story (5)

Down
1 Wanting food (6)
2 Poke (3)
3 Styles of clothes that people like (7)
5 The characters that make up the alphabet (7)
8 Small, rounded stone (6)
11 Obtained (3)

Puzzle: 66

Across
1 What can be seen right now (4)
4 Stop living (3)
5 Sound made by a cow (3)
6 Liquid used for writing (3)
8 Frequently (5)
9 The closing to a story, 'The ___' (3)
10 The closest star to Earth (3)
11 Liquid unit (5)
13 Try to get money from someone through a legal process (3)
15 Fish's eggs (3)
16 A group of objects belonging together (3)
17 Small water lizard (4)

Down
1 Underwear worn on your top half to keep you warm (4)
2 Came first in a race (3)
3 Glowing remains of a fire (6)
4 Quick sketch or drawing (6)
6 Put in (6)
7 House for a dog (6)
12 Check something (4)
14 Tall, rounded vase (3)

Puzzle: 67

Across
1 Shape associated with love (5)
3 Liquid food often made with vegetables and cream (4)
5 Strip of material worn around the neck to keep you warm (5)
8 Jam made with oranges (9)
9 Tap on a door (5)
11 Become in need of rest (4)
12 Elephants' tusks are made of this (5)

Down
1 Male equivalent of 'her' (3)
2 Mountain that erupts with molten lava (7)
4 Free of contamination (4)
6 Place where aeroplanes take off and land (7)
7 Container for keeping drinks hot or cold (5)
8 Watery ditch surrounding a castle (4)
10 Button on a computer (3)

Puzzle: 68

Across
1 Disgraceful (8)
5 For example: brazil, hazel, almond (3)
6 Sound made by a horse (5)
8 Fierce storm with strong winds (9)
10 Without anything missing (5)
13 Perform on stage (3)
15 The way in to a place (8)

Down
1 Break a law, especially a religious one (3)
2 Raised table in a church (5)
3 The cost for something (3)
4 Carry or drag something heavy (3)
6 Unpleasant sound (5)
7 Tool used for scraping up weeds (3)
8 In what way? (3)
9 Once more (5)
11 Tint; colour (3)
12 Large number (3)
14 Abbreviation for the day after Monday (3)

Puzzle: 69

Across
1 Picture painted on the wall (5)
4 Narrow end of something (3)
6 Model of a person used to scare birds away from crops (9)
7 Time between morning and evening (9)
10 Short for et cetera; 'and other things like this' (3)
11 The crime of stealing (5)

Down
1 Untidy state (4)
2 To do with love (8)
3 Similar to (4)
4 Slow creature with a shell (8)
5 Animal's foot (3)
7 Wonder (3)
8 Part of a plant that grows in the ground (4)
9 A bird's home (4)

Puzzle: 70

Across
4 Room under the roof of a house (5)
6 Green part of tree foliage (4)
7 Something a child plays with (3)
9 Yellow root vegetable (7)
10 Noah's ship for pairs of animals (3)
12 Snake noise (4)
13 Party where people dance (5)

Down
1 Trip to see wild animals in their natural homes (6)
2 A small part of something (3)
3 African big cat with spotted coat (7)
5 Decayed grass and leaves used to help plants grow (7)
8 Used to stop a boat from moving (6)
11 Family; relatives (3)

Puzzle: 71

Across
1 Tall tree with shiny bark (5)
3 Cover something in paper (4)
5 Girl's outfit (5)
8 Ninth month (9)
9 Sit down on your knees (5)
11 Poke or jab someone (4)
12 Powdery ice on the ground (5)

Down
1 Opposite of good (3)
2 Shake with fear (7)
4 Fruit grown on trees, narrower near the stalk (4)
6 For example: Julius Caesar or Augustus (7)
7 Thick slice of meat (5)
8 Cleaning substance (4)
10 Allow someone to do something (3)

Puzzle: 72

Across
1 Coloured part of the eye (4)
4 Evergreen tree with needle-like leaves (4)
7 Green citrus fruit, sometimes added to drinks (4)
8 Melody (4)
9 Spotty mushroom (9)
12 Fail to hit (4)
14 A large measure of land (4)
16 Cereal plant used for porridge (4)
17 A gap in something, such as clothing (4)

Down
1 Sick; not well (3)
2 How fast something moves (5)
3 Small, crawling insect (3)
5 Currency used in many European countries (4)
6 Basic unit of a living organism (4)
9 When describing animals, ____ is the opposite of 'wild' (4)
10 This as well; too (4)
11 Rubbish (5)
13 Tool with sharp teeth for cutting wood (3)
15 Two of these are used when you look at the world (3)

Puzzle: 73

Across
1 A repeated visual design (7)
6 Snake-shaped fish (3)
7 Christmas hymn (5)
8 Very tall flower with big yellow petals (9)
10 Time of day when you might see the moon (5)
12 Male equivalent of daughter (3)
13 Old-fashioned word for a snake (7)

Down
1 Colourful country bird with a long tail (8)
2 Strong claw, often found on a bird (5)
3 Often used to get from one floor to another in a shopping mall (9)
4 And not, as in 'neither this ___ that' (3)
5 Woodwind instrument (8)
9 Rubbish (5)
11 For example: oxygen or hydrogen (3)

Puzzle: 74

Across
1 Theatre show with sung music (5)
3 Stretched tight (4)
5 Sudden, bright light (5)
8 U-shaped piece of metal for a horse's hoof (9)
9 Let someone do something; permit (5)
11 Bucket (4)
12 Mix of yellow and blue (5)

Down
1 When I leave the house I set ___ (3)
2 Type of school bag (7)
4 Large plant with a trunk (4)
6 Post sent around the world by aeroplane (7)
7 Wild, wolf-like animal with wicked laugh (5)
8 Shout this to appeal for assistance (4)
10 Success; victory (3)

Puzzle: 75

Across
1 Not quick (4)
4 Available for business, especially if a shop (4)
7 A _ _ _ _ of shoes (4)
8 Something that you play (4)
9 Soft, cuddly toy (5,4)
12 For example: kitchen, lounge or hall (4)
14 For example: Henry VIII (4)
16 Law (4)
17 Boat made of logs tied together (4)

Down
1 Juice inside a tree (3)
2 The Earth and all its people (5)
3 Small barrel (3)
5 What a person is called (4)
6 Period of 365 days (4)
9 Pie containing jam (4)
10 Building entrance (4)
11 Someone who makes bread and cakes (5)
13 A big cup (3)
15 Remove insides from dead fish or animals (3)

Puzzle: 76

Across
4 Agreeable sounds made by instruments and voices (5)
6 Slightly wet (4)
7 Put money on the result of a game (3)
9 Dried grape; fruit used in a sweet bun (7)
10 A small wound (3)
12 Move in a circular direction (4)
13 Film seen at the cinema (5)

Down
1 Group of countries ruled by one person or country (6)
2 Metal point on a pen (3)
3 Milk contains _ _ _ _ _ _ _, which is good for bones and teeth (7)
5 One hundred years (7)
8 Person who serves food in a restaurant (6)
11 Heavy unit of weight (3)

Puzzle: 77

Across
1 School work you do at home (8)
5 Playground game where one person chases the rest (3)
6 Cleaning material (5)
8 A folding chair that you might take to the beach (9)
10 Fruit used for making wine (5)
13 Blockade across a river (3)
15 Felt curious about something (8)

Down
1 Covering for the head (3)
2 Tricks done by a performer to impress people (5)
3 Bird that calls 'too-wit too-woo' (3)
4 Clothes for sports (3)
6 Ride on a bicycle (5)
7 Female equivalent of 'his' (3)
8 Common family pet (3)
9 Small, poisonous snake (5)
11 A straight line of people (3)
12 Metal dish with a handle used for cooking (3)
14 Crazy; not sane (3)

Puzzle: 78

Across
1 Very small person (5)
3 Hard foot of a horse (4)
5 Newspapers and television in general (5)
8 White Arctic bear (5,4)
9 More than usual (5)
11 Place where a wild animal lives (4)
12 You dry your face or hands with this (5)

Down
1 Faintly lit (3)
2 Gather (7)
4 Number of sides a rectangle has (4)
6 Friendly sea animal with a fin (7)
7 Think the same as someone else (5)
8 Move something towards you (4)
10 The whole quantity of something (3)

Puzzle: 79

Across
1 Bumper car (6)
4 A gorilla, for example (3)
5 Added to (4)
7 Jump on one foot (3)
10 Clothing worn over the front of the body to protect clothes (5)
11 Home decorating (1,1,1)
13 Have to, as in 'you ____ do this' (4)
16 How something is done (3)
17 Hair accessory (6)

Down
1 Wild animal's home (3)
2 Briefly place something into a liquid and then take it back out (3)
3 Great unhappiness (6)
4 In the past; long ___ (3)
6 Country (4)
7 Tool for putting in nails (6)
8 Ticket in or out of a place (4)
9 Shed tears (3)
12 Slippery and cold (3)
14 Small flap used to mark a page (3)
15 Belonging to you (3)

Puzzle: 80

Across
4 Sudden feeling of fear (5)
6 Thin metal sheet used for cooking (4)
7 Cardboard container (3)
9 Small falcon (7)
10 Stitch together with a needle and thread (3)
12 Write your signature (4)
13 The main part of your body (5)

Down
1 If you jump into a swimming pool, you will make a _____ (6)
2 Tell a lie (3)
3 Small book with paper covers (7)
5 A picture made by sticking scraps of paper together (7)
8 Jail (6)
11 Deep frying pan used to make Chinese food (3)

Puzzle: 81

Across
1 Small bird with a short, thick beak (5)
3 Repeatedly hit the palms of your hands together (4)
5 What you turn to steer a vehicle (5)
8 Every person (9)
9 Large vehicle for moving goods (5)
11 Long, pointed tooth of an elephant (4)
12 Taking a short time (5)

Down
1 More than one but less than several (3)
2 Taste (7)
4 Small horse (4)
6 Short hair on your eyelid (7)
7 Faithful (5)
8 The way out (4)
10 Long-haired ox (3)

Puzzle: 82

Across
1 Slightly open (4)
3 Mixture of smoke and fog (4)
5 Short hairs on a man's chin (7)
9 Rules of a country (3)
10 Stand used by artists for a painting (5)
11 To be able; 'I ___ do this' (3)
12 Itch with fingernails (7)
16 Give food to a person (4)
17 Connects devices to electricity (4)

Down
1 The horns on a deer (7)
2 Rodent that resembles a large mouse (3)
3 Cry uncontrollably (3)
4 Thick liquid used for cooking (3)
5 Make a promise (5)
6 Anxious; worried (5)
7 Burp (5)
8 Time when the sun sets (7)
13 Stick used to play pool or billiards (3)
14 A joining word, as in 'this ___ that' (3)
15 Slang term for a police officer (3)

Puzzle: 83

Across
1 Hard covering over a healing cut or graze (4)
4 Uncut bread (4)
7 Hair on the neck of a horse or lion (4)
8 Primary painting colour (4)
9 Rough paper used to smooth wood (9)
12 Specific day in history when something happened (4)
14 Hold on to (4)
16 Bad or wicked (4)
17 The direction in which the sun rises (4)

Down
1 The result of adding some numbers (3)
2 Mix together smoothly (5)
3 Taxi (3)
5 Turn over quickly (4)
6 For example: grizzly, polar or teddy (4)
9 Another word for 'team' in football (4)
10 Something you write to help you remember things (4)
11 Joint connecting your leg to your foot (5)
13 Evening before an important day (3)
15 Place something somewhere (3)

Puzzle: 84

Across
1 A pale colour (6)
4 A long way (3)
5 Something designed to catch you out (4)
7 To and ___; going backwards and forwards (3)
10 The colour of earth (5)
11 Space between two things (3)
13 A plant growing where it isn't wanted (4)
16 Large tree with acorns (3)
17 The magician pulled a _____ out of his hat! (6)

Down
1 Be nosy (3)
2 Took a seat (3)
3 Small, portable computer (6)
4 On behalf of (3)
6 Finger jewellery (4)
7 Colourful part of a plant (6)
8 Woodwind instrument (4)
9 Place where wild animals are kept for people to see (3)
12 Question someone (3)
14 Touch gently with a tissue in order to clean or dry (3)
15 Note down quickly (3)

Puzzle: 85

Across
1 Pack things tightly into a space (3)
3 Place where scientists work (3)
5 I am, he is, you ___ (3)
7 Look unusually pale or ill (3)
8 Fame; honour (5)
10 Flying vehicle with wings and an engine (9)
13 Useful (5)
16 Small container for food (3)
18 Tool for chopping wood (3)
19 Bite sharply, like a dog might do (3)
20 Colour of a stop light (3)

Down
1 Lower, movable part of the face (3)
2 Large country house with grounds (5)
3 Part of the body between the feet and the hips (3)
4 Noise made by a ghost (3)
6 Ancient instrument, like a small harp (4)
9 Text speak for 'laughing out loud' (abbreviation) (1,1,1)
10 A steady pain (4)
11 Opposite of even (3)
12 Make a change (5)
14 Religious woman (3)
15 Small barking sound (3)
17 Something you sleep on (3)

Puzzle: 86

Across
4 Book of maps (5)
6 Melt from frozen (4)
7 Joined someone at an agreed place (3)
9 Chief law officer in US counties (7)
10 Shown where to go (3)
12 Cage or house for chickens (4)
13 To do with kings and queens (5)

Down
1 Solicitor; expert in legal matters (6)
2 Tropical vegetable, like a potato (3)
3 Hair on an animal's face (7)
5 Edible fish or shellfish (7)
8 Perfectly-round shape (6)
11 Female deer (3)

Puzzle: 87

Across
1 Opposite of stale (5)
4 Gave food to (3)
6 Spying; the use of spies (9)
7 Dark-coloured songbird (9)
10 Fetch; obtain (3)
11 Opposite of long (5)

Down
1 Something that is burning is on ____ (4)
2 Large, grey animal with big ears and a trunk (8)
3 Person who does something brave (4)
4 Pink wading bird (8)
5 Planned for a certain time (3)
7 Larger than normal size (3)
8 Lovingly touch someone with your lips (4)
9 Special food programme; it's important to eat a balanced ____ (4)

Puzzle: 88

Across
1 Yellow food made from almonds and sugar (8)
5 Pester or repeatedly complain to someone (3)
6 Father Christmas (5)
8 Tried (9)
10 To march, long and far (5)
13 Highest part of something (3)
15 A one-floor house (8)

Down
1 Grown-up male person (3)
2 Opposite of left (5)
3 Small round green vegetable that grows in a pod (3)
4 The opposite of something, as in 'I will do this but ___ that' (3)
6 To summarize something (3,2)
7 The opposite of 'subtract' (3)
8 Appropriate; suitable (3)
9 The result of adding up some numbers (5)
11 Steal something (3)
12 Plural of 'man' (3)
14 Wooden bench in a church (3)

Puzzle: 89

Across
4 Special prize given for achievement (5)
6 Large shellfish with two shells of equal size (4)
7 The number of fingers and thumbs you have (3)
9 Whirlwind (7)
10 For each, as in 'one ___ person' (3)
12 Joy; delight (4)
13 In the countryside (5)

Down
1 Photo-taking device (6)
2 For example: drawings, paintings, sculptures and music (3)
3 Shiny, powdery substance used in crafts (7)
5 Loving; loyal (7)
8 Twist string together (6)
11 What Aladdin did to the lamp (3)

Puzzle: 90

Across
1 Book for collecting photos or stamps (5)
3 Illuminates a room (4)
5 Symbol used to indicate subtraction (5)
8 Group of people living in one place (9)
9 Not clean (5)
11 Place where pigs and cows are often kept (4)
12 Piece of paper (5)

Down
1 Limb connected to your shoulder (3)
2 Someone who fights in battle (7)
4 A theatre show (4)
6 1, 2 and 3 are _____ (7)
7 Something you can hear (5)
8 A part of your leg, below the knee (4)
10 It hasn't happened ___ (3)

Puzzle: 91

Across
1 White bony parts in your mouth (5)
4 Large piece of wood from a fallen tree (3)
6 A way to cook eggs (9)
7 Mark left by a step (9)
10 Opposite of no (3)
11 Someone taught by a teacher (5)

Down
1 Something children play with (4)
2 Very big (8)
3 Hurt or damage someone (4)
4 Hard candy on a stick (8)
5 Deity; a being that is worshipped (3)
7 Cook in hot fat (3)
8 Object used on stage in a theatre (4)
9 Work hard (4)

Puzzle: 92

Across
1 Deep breath of relief or sadness (4)
4 Make changes (4)
7 British nobleman (4)
8 Medicine (4)
9 Instrument often used to play jazz (9)
12 Level; smooth (4)
14 Young sheep; Mary had a little ____ (4)
16 Large piece of material on a ship, used to catch the wind (4)
17 Indian style of meditation (4)

Down
1 Look at something with your eyes (3)
2 Opposite of goodbye (5)
3 Child (3)
5 Group of three people (4)
6 Large, cruel giant (4)
9 Opposite of hard (4)
10 Short for 'Christmas' (4)
11 Spiky Christmas plant with red berries (5)
13 Money that must be paid to the government (3)
15 Sound made by a sheep (3)

Puzzle: 93

Across
4 Poisonous (5)
6 Small jumping insect (4)
7 Cut grass with a machine (3)
9 Someone who studies at university (7)
10 Used for cleaning floors (3)
12 Great anger (4)
13 Damp; slightly wet (5)

Down
1 Carved model of a person or animal (6)
2 Point at a target (3)
3 Flowers growing on a fruit tree (7)
5 Small house in the country (7)
8 Red playing card suit (6)
11 Seed container (3)

Puzzle: 94

Across
1 Small, common flower with white petals and a yellow centre (5)
3 Place where you can buy things (4)
5 Flow of water onto a beach (5)
8 Large, tropical fruit with prickly skin (9)
9 Before second and third (5)
11 Used for keeping money in a shop (4)
12 Shellfish, like a large shrimp (5)

Down
1 Drops of water formed on cool surfaces during the night (3)
2 Speak softly (7)
4 Sheet of glass in a window (4)
6 'Plain' ice cream flavour (7)
7 People who work in an office (5)
8 Some but not all (4)
10 Metal container (3)

Puzzle: 95

Across
1 Centre of a wheel (3)
3 Public transport vehicle (3)
5 Used to refer to one or more of something, as in '___ quantity' (3)
7 A waterproof coat (3)
8 All of something (5)
10 Small orange (9)
13 Italian noodles (5)
16 Help (3)
18 Practical joke (3)
19 Pastry dish filled with meat or fruit (3)
20 A Muslim festival (3)

Down
1 Cooked meat from a pig (3)
2 Salted meat from a pig (5)
3 Casual goodbye (3)
4 Female equivalent of 'he' (3)
6 A unit of computer memory storage (4)
9 Video cassette recorder (abbreviation) (1,1,1)
10 Write on a computer keyboard (4)
11 Obtained (3)
12 Picture (5)
14 A small quantity of a drink (3)
15 The length of time that a person has been alive (3)
17 Disc with a film or TV show on it (1,1,1)

Puzzle: 96

Across
1 Nervous; easily frightened (5)
4 Wipe your feet on this (3)
6 Big, hairy spider (9)
7 Long, stringy pasta (9)
10 Substance used to colour hair or clothes (3)
11 Appears when you rub a lamp in some fairy tales (5)

Down
1 Printed words (4)
2 The permanent joining of two adults (8)
3 Opposite of up (4)
4 Very high hill with a peak (8)
5 Meal eaten in the afternoon (3)
7 Opposite of happy (3)
8 The Christmas decorations were ____ on the tree (4)
9 Lazy (4)

Puzzle: 97

Across
1 A person, as distinguished from other animals (5)
3 Hut for storing gardening tools (4)
5 Rest in bed (5)
8 Paper used to cover room walls (9)
9 Underground part of a tree (5)
11 Job that needs to be done (4)
12 Cereal plant used to make flour (5)

Down
1 Male equivalent of 'her' (3)
2 Soap for washing your hair (7)
4 Forest grazing animal with hooves (4)
6 Shadow of the moon against the sun (7)
7 Thin material used for writing on (5)
8 Direction in which the sun sets (4)
10 Rest your bottom on a chair (3)

Puzzle: 98

Across
1 Unusual (8)
5 Paddle used to row a boat (3)
6 Tool used to dig (5)
8 Strong wind which spins everything around (9)
10 Weapon with a long, pointed blade (5)
13 Opposite of high (3)
15 Heavy fall of rain (8)

Down
1 Alien spaceship (1,1,1)
2 The Queen's favourite little dog (5)
3 Details of the roads and land in an area (3)
4 Head movement used to agree (3)
6 Healthy mix of cold, raw vegetables (5)
7 The point where something stops (3)
8 Used to be (3)
9 House made of ice (5)
11 Bundle of soft material (3)
12 Uncooked (3)
14 Time of conflict (3)

COLOUR BY NUMBERS

1 = grey   2 = blue   3 = dark green   4 = light green   5 = yellow
6 = orange   7 = red   8 = purple

1 = light blue   2 = dark blue   3 = red   4 = yellow   5 = brown
6 = light green   7 = dark green

DOODLING

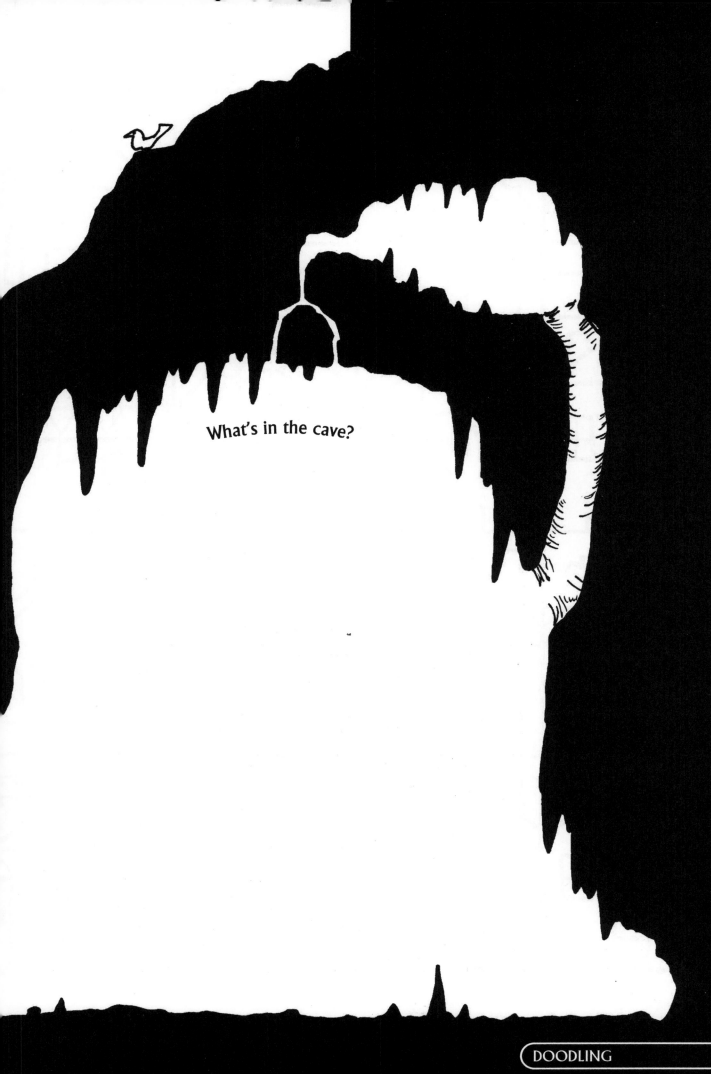

What's in the cave?

1 = yellow   2 = red   3 = pink   4 = orange   5 = light blue   6 = dark blue

1 = dark blue   2 = light blue   3 = yellow   4 = orange   5 = pink   6 = purple

WORDSEARCHES

This section is full of wordsearches. Beneath each puzzle is a list of words that are hidden in the grid above it. You'll find the words running in a straight line in any direction, including diagonally, and either forwards or backwards.

Occasionally, some of the puzzles contain a phrase or word written beneath the grid that includes punctuation – in these cases just ignore the spaces or punctuation marks when looking in the grid. When you find a word, mark it in the grid and cross it off the list below. Some of the puzzles have interesting shapes with lines drawn between the letters in the grid – ignore these when solving the puzzles, since the words can still run across these lines.

You should also remember that some of the words in each puzzle will overlap one another – using the same letters in the grid.

The wordsearches get harder as you work through the section. If you get completely stuck and can't find a word, don't panic – all of the answers are in the back of the book.

Puzzle 1: Let's Face It

CHEEKS		FOREHEAD
CHIN		MOUTH
EARS		NOSE
EYEBROWS		NOSTRILS
EYELASHES		TEETH
EYES		TONGUE

Puzzle 2: What's That Taste?

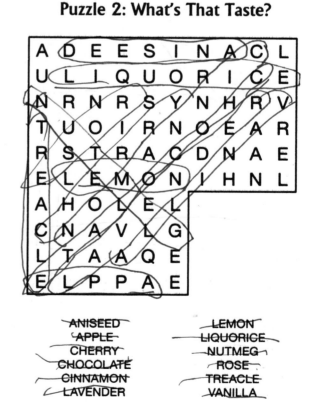

ANISEED		LEMON
APPLE		LIQUORICE
CHERRY		NUTMEG
CHOCOLATE		ROSE
CINNAMON		TREACLE
LAVENDER		VANILLA

Puzzle 3: Cake

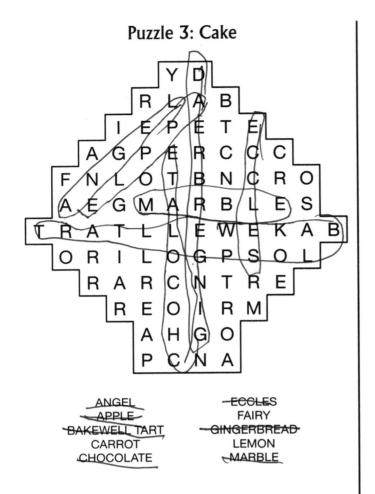

```
              Y D
          R L A B
        I E P E T E
      A G P E R C C C
    F N L O T B N C R O
  A E G M A R B L E S
T R A T L L E W E K A B
  O R I L O G P S O L
    R A R C N T R E
      R E O I R M
        A H G O
          P C N A
```

ANGEL
APPLE
BAKEWELL TART
CARROT
CHOCOLATE

ECCLES
FAIRY
GINGERBREAD
LEMON
MARBLE

Puzzle 4: Girls' Names

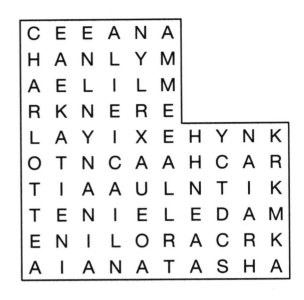

```
C E E A N A
H A N L Y M
A E L I L M
R K N E R E
L A Y I X E H Y N K
O T N C A A H C A R
T I A A U L N T I K
T E N I E L E D A M
E N I L O R A C R K
A I A N A T A S H A
```

ALEXANDRA   KATHERINE
ANNA   KATIE
CAROLINE   KAY
CHARLOTTE   LUCY
ELAINE   MADELEINE
EMMA   MICHELLE
KATE   NATASHA

Puzzle 5: Meal Time

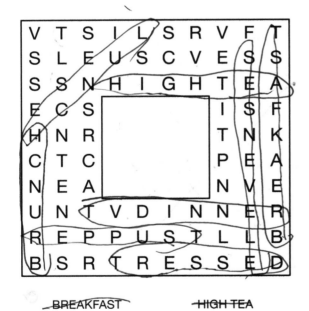

```
V T S I L S R V F T
S L E U S C V E S S
S S N H I G H T E A
E C S         I S F
H N R         T N K
C T C         P E A
N E A         N V E
U N T V D I N N E R
R E P P U S T L L B
B S R T R E S S E D
```

BREAKFAST   HIGH TEA
BRUNCH   LUNCH
DESSERT   SUPPER
ELEVENSES   TV DINNER

Puzzle 6: Month Mix-Up

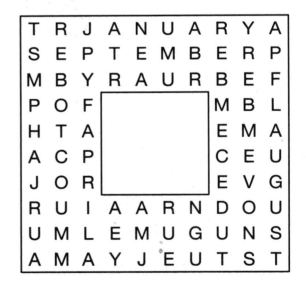

```
T R J A N U A R Y A
S E P T E M B E R P
M B Y R A U R B E F
P O F         M B L
H T A         E M A
A C P         C E U
J O R         E V G
R U I A A R N D O U
U M L E M U G U N S
A M A Y J E U T S T
```

APRIL   JUNE
AUGUST   MARCH
DECEMBER   MAY
FEBRUARY   NOVEMBER
JANUARY   OCTOBER
JULY   SEPTEMBER

Puzzle 7: Counties In England

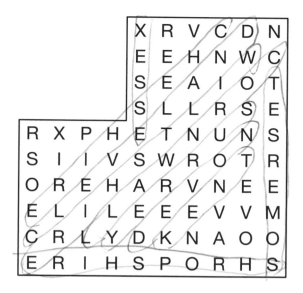

```
X R V C D N
E E H N W C
S E A I O T
S L L R S E
R X P H E T N U N S
S I I V S W R O T R
O R E H A R V N E E
E L I L E E E V V M
C R L Y D K N A O O
E R I H S P O R H S
```

CHESHIRE   KENT
CLEVELAND   SHROPSHIRE
CORNWALL   SOMERSET
DEVON   SURREY
ESSEX   WILTSHIRE

Puzzle 8: Juicy Jumble

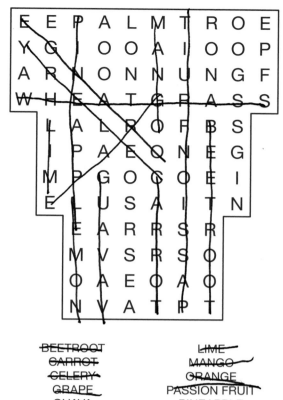

```
E E P A L M T R O E
Y G O O A I O O P
A R N O N N U N G F
W H E A T G R A S S
   L A L R O F B S
   I P A E Q N E G
   M P G O G O E I
   E L U S A I T N
   E A R R S R
   M V S R S O
   O A E O A O
   N V A T P T
```

BEETROOT   LIME
CARROT   MANGO
CELERY   ORANGE
GRAPE   PASSION FRUIT
GUAVA   PINEAPPLE
LEMON   WHEATGRASS

Puzzle 9: Getting Washed

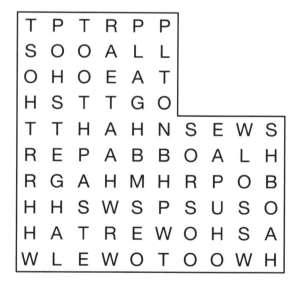

```
T P T R P P
S O O A L L
O H O E A T
H S T T G O
T T H A H N S E W S
R E P A B B O A L H
R G A H M H R P O B
H H S W S P S U S O
H A T R E W O H S A
W L E W O T O O W H
```

BATH   SPONGE
LATHER   TOOTHBRUSH
SHAMPOO   TOOTHPASTE
SHOWER   TOWEL
SOAP   WASH

Puzzle 10: The World of Roald Dahl

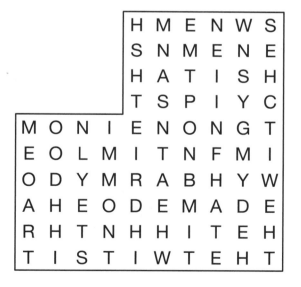

```
         H M E N W S
         S N M E N E
         H A T I S H
         T S P I Y C
M O N I E N O N G T
E O L M I T N F M I
O D Y M R A B H Y W
A H E O D E M A D E
R H T N H H I T E H
T I S T I W T E H T
```

DANNY   THE BFG
ESIO TROT   THE MINPINS
MATILDA   THE TWITS
RHYME STEW   THE WITCHES

Puzzle 11: Emperors

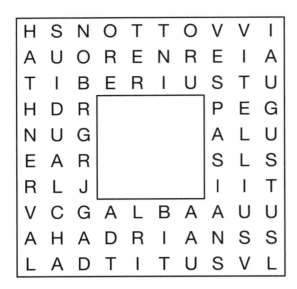

```
H S N O T T O V V I
A U O R E N R E I A
T I B E R I U S T U
H D R     P E G
N U G     A L U
E A R     S L S
R L J       I I T
V C G A L B A A U U
A H A D R I A N S S
L A D T I T U S V L
```

AUGUSTUS
CLAUDIUS
GALBA
HADRIAN
NERO
NERVA

OTTO
TIBERIUS
TITUS
TRAJAN
VESPASIAN
VITELLIUS

Puzzle 12: Christmas Time

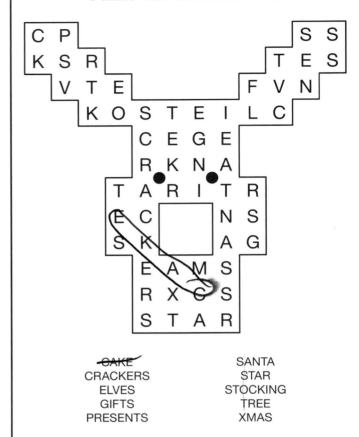

CAKE
CRACKERS
ELVES
GIFTS
PRESENTS

SANTA
STAR
STOCKING
TREE
XMAS

Puzzle 13: Healthy Eating

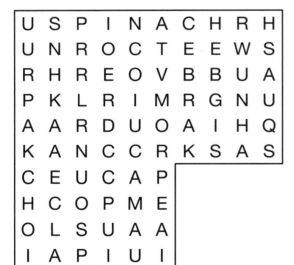

```
U S P I N A C H R H
U N R O C T E E W S
R H R E O V B B U A
P K L R I M R G N U
A A R D U O A I H Q
K A N C C R K S A S
C E U C A P
H C O P M E
O L S U A A
I A P I U I
```

ASPARAGUS
BROCCOLI
CARROT
CUCUMBER
ENDIVE
KALE

PAK CHOI
PEA
PUMPKIN
SPINACH
SQUASH
SWEETCORN

Puzzle 14: Art Attack

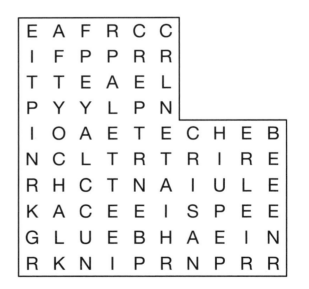

```
E A F R C C
I F P P R R
T T E A E L
P Y Y L P N
I O A E T E C H E B
N C L T R T R I R E
R H C T N A I U L E
K A C E E I S P E E
G L U E B H A E I N
R K N I P R N P R R
```

BRUSH
CHALK
CLAY
CRAYON
ERASER
FELT TIP

GLUE
INK
PAINT
PALETTE
PAPER
PENCIL

Puzzle 15: Body Boggle

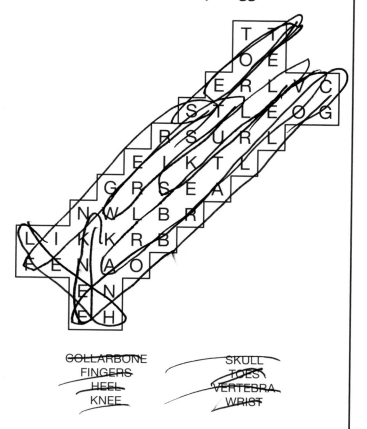

		T	T			
		O	E			
	E	R	L	V	C	
	S	T	E	O	G	
	R	S	U	R	L	
	E	L	K	T	L	
	G	R	S	E	A	
	N	W	L	B	R	
L	I	K	K	R	B	
E	E	N	A	O		
			E	N		
			E	H		

COLLARBONE   SKULL
FINGERS   TOES
HEEL   VERTEBRA
KNEE   WRIST

Puzzle 16: Big Cats

B	X	W	T	I	G	E	R	S	R
N	B	N	I	J	A	G	U	A	R
C	O	C	E	L	O	T	C	N	X
O	B	I	H	S	D	O	A	D	P
L	C	Y	L	E	U	C	R	C	A
O	A	J	A	G	E	A	A	A	N
N	T	M	A	G	P	T	C	T	T
H	U	R	Y	O	R	P	A	H	H
P	G	S	E	R	V	A	L	H	E
B	R	L	Y	N	X	R	M	H	R

BOBCAT	MARGAY
CARACAL	OCELOT
CHEETAH	PANTHER
COUGAR	PUMA
JAGUAR	SAND CAT
LEOPARD	SERVAL
LION	TIGER
LYNX	WILDCAT

Puzzle 17: United Kingdom Rivers

C	N	P	W	N	R	E	V	E	S
L	D	N	A	V	O	N	E	N	E
Y	E	I	A	Y	A	W	D	E	M
D	R	R	I	B	B	L	E	E	A
E	S	U	O	T	A	E	R	G	H
U	Y	E	P	S	R	S	W	D	T
			E	E	E	E	Y	I
			Y	M	E	N	R	W
			A	W	E	T	T	U
			T	R	E	T	E	S

AIRE	MERSEY	TEME
AVON	NENE	THAMES
BANN	RIBBLE	TRENT
CLYDE	SEVERN	TWEED
DERWENT	SPEY	TYNE
GREAT OUSE	TAY	URE
MEDWAY	TEES	WITHAM

Puzzle 18: The Name Game

		R	B	H	M	B	U
		M	A	D	A	M	D
		M	M	R	S	A	U
		N	O	D	T	R	C
T	I	Q	E	N	U	L	E	Q	H
E	E	E	K	K	A	T	R	U	E
A	U	A	E	I	S	I	R	E	S
Q	E	P	R	I	N	C	E	S	S
S	O	D	M	L	U	G	N	S	I
N	V	I	S	C	O	U	N	T	M

BARON	MADAM	QUEEN
DUCHESS	MARQUESS	SIR
DUKE	MASTER	VISCOUNT
EARL	MISS	
KING	MRS	
LAIRD	PRINCESS	

Puzzle 19: Playing Chess

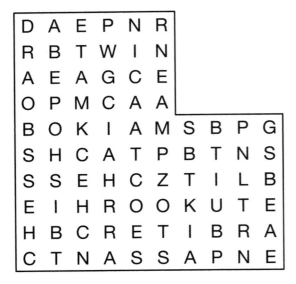

D	A	E	P	N	R
R	B	T	W	I	N
A	E	A	G	C	E
O	P	M	C	A	A
B	O	K	I	A	M	S	B	P	G
S	H	C	A	T	P	B	T	N	S
S	S	E	H	C	Z	T	I	L	B
E	I	H	R	O	O	K	U	T	E
H	B	C	R	E	T	I	B	R	A
C	T	N	A	S	S	A	P	N	E

ARBITER
BISHOP
BLITZ CHESS
CAPTURE
CASTLE
CHECKMATE
CHESSBOARD

EN PASSANT
GAMBIT
KING
PAWN
ROOK
TIMER
WIN

Puzzle 20: Medical Attention

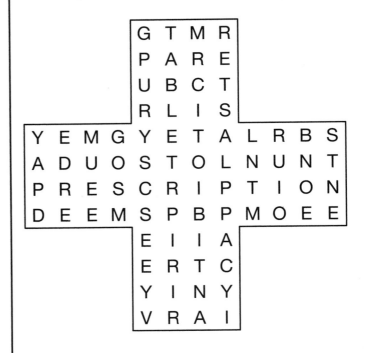

ANTIBIOTIC
DRUG
PILL
PLASTER
PRESCRIPTION

REMEDY
SYRUP
TABLET
TISSUE
VITAMINS

Puzzle 21: Time For Fun

G	L	L	A	B	T	O	O	F	V
M	R	E	A	D	I	N	G	T	C
S	W	R	I	T	I	N	G	O	G
E	I	N	D	L	I	N	M	N	E
L	A	S	A	T	I	P	I	A	I
Z	I	Z	N	H	U	M	L	O	L
Z	E	I	C	T	M
U	A	T	E	I	R
P	A	R	W	I	L
W	S	S	T	C	D

ART
COMPUTERS
DANCE
FOOTBALL

PAINTING
PUZZLES
READING
SWIMMING

WATCHING TV
WRITING

Puzzle 22: Numbers, Big And Small

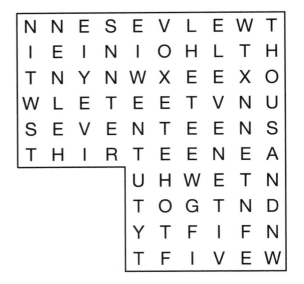

N	N	E	S	E	V	L	E	W	T
I	E	I	N	I	O	H	L	T	H
T	N	Y	N	W	X	E	E	X	O
W	L	E	T	E	E	T	V	N	U
S	E	V	E	N	T	E	E	N	S
T	H	I	R	T	E	E	N	E	A
				U	H	W	E	T	N
				T	O	G	T	N	D
				Y	T	F	I	F	N
				T	F	I	V	E	W

EIGHTEEN
ELEVEN
FIFTY
FIVE
FOUR

NINETEEN
ONE
SEVENTEEN
SIXTEEN
THIRTEEN

THOUSAND
TWELVE
TWENTY
TWO

Puzzle 23: Things You Put On The Wall

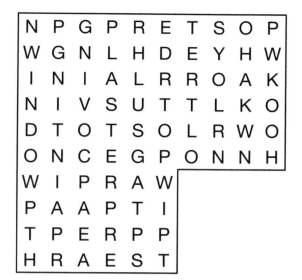

N	P	G	P	R	E	T	S	O	P
W	G	N	L	H	D	E	Y	H	W
I	N	I	A	L	R	R	O	A	K
N	I	V	S	U	T	T	L	K	O
D	T	O	T	S	O	L	R	W	O
O	N	C	E	G	P	O	N	N	H
W	I	P	R	A	W
P	A	A	P	T	I
T	P	E	R	P	P
H	R	A	E	S	T

ARTWORK
COVING
HOOK
PAINTING
PHOTOGRAPH
PICTURE

PLASTER
POSTER
SIGN
TAPESTRY
WALLPAPER
WINDOW

Puzzle 24: Fluffy Animals

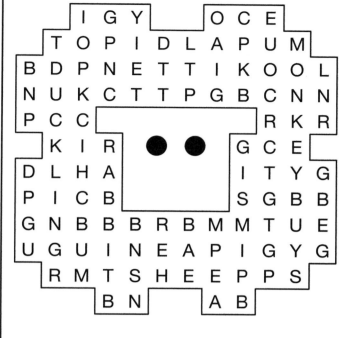

BEAR
CAT
CHICK
CUB
DOG

DUCKLING
GERBIL
GUINEA PIG
HAMSTER
KITTEN

MONKEY
PUPPY
RABBIT
SHEEP

Puzzle 25: All At Sea

S	O	U	T	H	C	H	I	N	A
A	N	A	R	A	B	I	A	N	C
N	A	P	A	J	H	E	I	I	K
A	M	R	T	T	B	H	T	S	A
I	A	E	R	B	C	A	T	I	P
P	D	O	I	T	I	O	A	A	L
S	N	R	S	R	H
A	A	A	D	K	C
C	E	A	O	E	R
K	C	A	L	B	R

ADRIATIC
ANDAMAN
ARABIAN
BLACK
CARIBBEAN
CASPIAN

EAST CHINA
JAPAN
NORTH
OKHOTSK
RED
SOUTH CHINA

Puzzle 26: Scary Monsters

O	U	G	H	O	U	L	P	A	I
A	P	E	U	N	D	E	A	D	M
H	Z	H	V	R	I	C	T	O	O
C	O	E	A	B	T	T	N	B	S
T	D	Z	M	N	I	S	A	P	Z
I	I	O	P	R	T	N	O	P	I
W	Z	A	I	E	S	O	H	H	P
N	S	P	R	H	K	O	M	R	G
R	S	P	E	C	T	R	E	P	U
C	W	E	R	E	W	O	L	F	S

BANSHEE
GHOST
GHOUL
MONSTER
PHANTOM
SPECTRE
SPIRIT

SPOOK
UNDEAD
VAMPIRE
WEREWOLF
WITCH
WIZARD
ZOMBIE

Puzzle 27: Team Sports

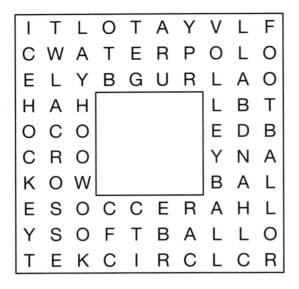

I	T	L	O	T	A	Y	V	L	F
C	W	A	T	E	R	P	O	L	O
E	L	Y	B	G	U	R	L	A	O
H	A	H					L	B	T
O	C	O					E	D	B
C	R	O					Y	N	A
K	O	W					B	A	L
E	S	O	C	C	E	R	A	H	L
Y	S	O	F	T	B	A	L	L	O
T	E	K	C	I	R	C	L	C	R

CRICKET   RUGBY
FOOTBALL   SOCCER
HANDBALL   SOFTBALL
ICE HOCKEY   VOLLEYBALL
LACROSSE   WATER POLO

Puzzle 28: Toy Box

CARDS   PUZZLE
DOLLS   SLINKY
JIGSAW   SPINNING TOP
KITE   TOY CARS
MODEL   TRAIN SET

Puzzle 29: Athletics

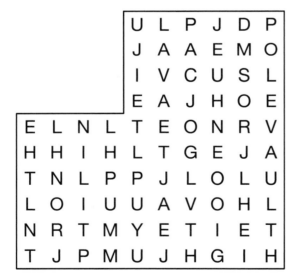

DECATHLON   POLE VAULT
HIGH JUMP   RELAY
JAVELIN   SHOT PUT
LONG JUMP   TRIPLE JUMP

Puzzle 30: Natural Water Features

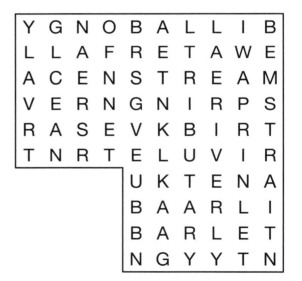

BAY   REEF   STREAM
BILLABONG   RIVER   TARN
CREEK   RIVULET   TRIBUTARY
ESTUARY   SEA   WATERFALL
INLET   SPRING
LAKE   STRAIT

Puzzle 31: Woodwind Instruments

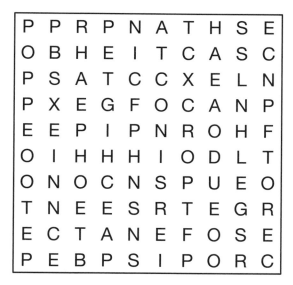

```
P P R P N A T H S E
O B H E I T C A S C
P S A T C C X E L N
P X E G F O C A N P
E E P I P N R O H F
O I H H H I O D L T
O N O C N S P U E O
T N E E S R T E G R
E C T A N E F O S E
P E B P S I P O R C
```

BAGPIPES
BASSOON
CLARINET
FLUTE

HORNPIPE
PICCOLO
RECORDER
SAXOPHONE

Puzzle 32: Breakfast Feast

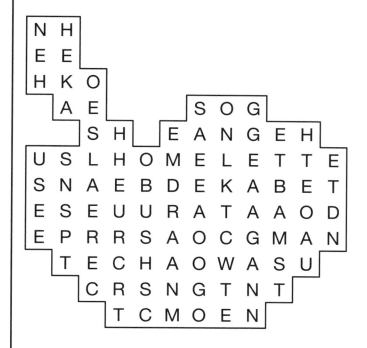

```
N H
E E
H K O
  A E     S O G
  S H   E A N G E H
U S L H O M E L E T T E
S N A E B D E K A B E T
E S E U U R A T A A O D
E P R R S A O C G M A N
  T E C H A O W A S U
  C R S N G T N T
  T C M O E N
```

BACON
BAKED BEANS
CEREAL
CREPE
EGG

HASH BROWN
OMELETTE
SAUSAGE
TOAST
TOMATO

Puzzle 33: Power Crazy

```
E G O G V D O I G W
S A F N U C L E A R
H S L L O N N V F L
U Y A L C I E U E I
P O D M B N S S D O
C R W R O I E S N V
L E U F O I B S I U
F T E N D G B E W F
L S L O R T E P L B
O O I I V O D N C D
```

BIOFUEL
BIOMASS
COAL
DIESEL
FISSION
FUSION
GAS

HYDROGEN
NUCLEAR
OIL
PETROL
TURBINE
WAVE
WIND

Puzzle 34: Drink Up!

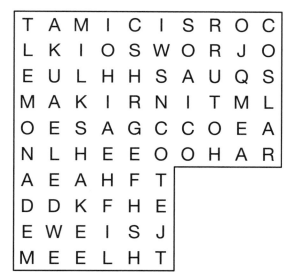

```
T A M I C I S R O C
L K I O S W O R J O
E U L H H S A U Q S
M A K I R N I T M L
O E S A G C C O E A
N L H E E O O H A R
A E A H F T
D D K F H E
E W E I S J
M E E L H T
```

COFFEE
COLA
JUICE
LEMONADE
MILKSHAKE

ORANGEADE
SMOOTHIE
SQUASH
TEA
WATER

Puzzle 35: Farmyard Fun

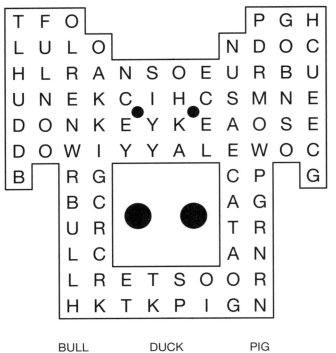

BULL
CALF
CAT
CHICKEN
COW
DONKEY

DUCK
GOAT
GOOSE
HEN
HORSE
LAMB

PIG
ROOSTER
SHEEP
TURKEY

Puzzle 36: Christian Saints

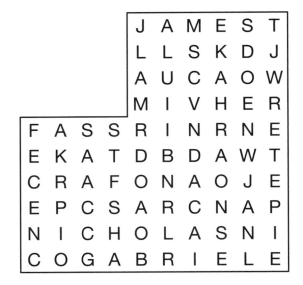

ANDREW
ANNE
DAVID
ERASMUS
GABRIEL
JAMES

JOAN OF ARC
JOHN BOSCO
NICHOLAS
PANCRAS
PATRICK
PETER

Puzzle 37: Sandwich Selection

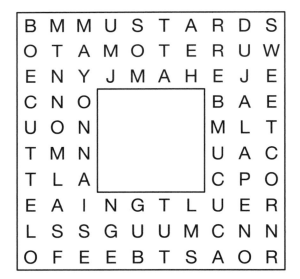

CLUB
CUCUMBER
EGG
HAM
JALAPENO
JAM
LETTUCE

MAYONNAISE
MUSTARD
ROAST BEEF
SALMON
SWEETCORN
TOMATO
TUNA

Puzzle 38: Shades Of Green

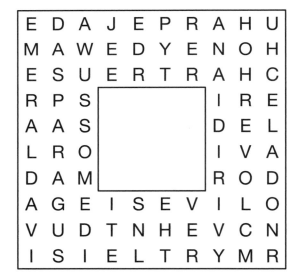

ASPARAGUS
CELADON
CHARTREUSE
CLOVER
EMERALD
HONEYDEW
JADE

MINT
MOSS
MYRTLE
OLIVE
PEAR
TEAL
VIRIDIAN

Puzzle 39: In The Back Garden

```
          L S S R R S
          A S E E R T
          W G L S P O
          N K B P A B
H B S U N B A T H E
E E O I U V T P T Z
R L R S I W E A H A
B P H N O S G A A G
S E G M O R E T A W
B U R H S E V A E L
```

BUSH
GATE
GAZEBO
HERBS
HOSE
LAWN
LEAVES
LOUNGER
MOW
PAVING
SHRUB
SPRINKLER
SUNBATHE
TREES
VEGETABLES
WATER

Puzzle 40: Biscuit Crackers

```
I T S J D P O A R I A T
S D U R A L E Z T E R P
L H L N E F Z R T K W I
J A O A R I F H A A P E
P N R R B E C A F C M V
U O E L T I G E C T T I
R O K S R C R N R A A T
O R C A O E A A I O K S
T A A H H R H K G G R E
E C R I S P B R E A D G
E A C L N O B R U O B I
R M S F L A P J A C K D
```

BOURBON
CRACKER
CRISPBREAD
DIGESTIVE
FLAPJACK
GARIBALDI
GINGER NUT
JAFFA CAKE
MACAROON
MATZO
OATCAKE
PRETZEL
RICH TEA
SHORTBREAD
SHORTCAKE
WAFER

Puzzle 41: Shades Of Blue

```
D E S I O U Q R U T N A
L C U A G L A U C O U S
C M Y C I T Z N T I A E
O I D A D R U E L P L R
B D N M N A R E P K E N
A N A B I M E H N D A C
L I I R M A I I W E A U
T G S I S R W O L U E A
E H S D E I P U
G T U G R N R P
R R R E H E R I
I U P U C Y R D
```

AZURE
CAMBRIDGE
CERULEAN
COBALT
CYAN
ETON
GLAUCOUS
INDIGO
IRIS
MIDNIGHT
PERIWINKLE
POWDER
PRUSSIAN
SAPPHIRE
TURQUOISE
ULTRAMARINE

Puzzle 42: On The Computer

```
C N R E O L K R P C R R
R A N E T W O R K O C R
O T D D B T E R D Y A R
I E M E I T D V R T B T
L K V N N T D O C H L O
B D O I A D M T R C E D
M M R B R E N N A C S B
N P L I M D N N N I U K
A E V I R D D C N K O I
T E N O H P O R C I M M
N L M K E Y B O A R D T
I I I N D I D A N H A T
```

CABLE
CD-DRIVE
DOCK
DVD-DRIVE
HARD-DRIVE
KEYBOARD
MEMORY
MICROPHONE
MONITOR
MOUSE
NETWORK
PRINTER
SCANNER
TABLET

Puzzle 43: Dinner Time

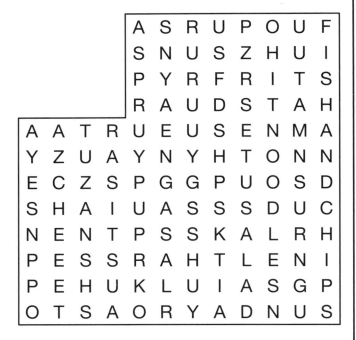

```
        A S R U P O U F
        S N U S Z H U I
        P Y R F R I T S
        R A U D S T A H
A A T R U E U S E N M A
Y Z U A Y N Y H T O N N
E C Z S P G G P U O S D
S H A I U A S S S D U C
N E N T P S S K A L R H
P E S S R A H T L E N I
P E H U K L U I A S G P
O T S A O R Y A D N U S
```

CURRY	PASTA	SUNDAY
FISH AND	PIZZA	ROAST
CHIPS	SALAD	SUSHI
LASAGNE	SOUP	TAPAS
MOUSSAKA	SPAGHETTI	
NOODLES	STIR FRY	

Puzzle 44: They're All Teachers!

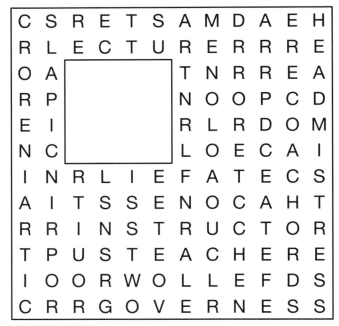

```
C S R E T S A M D A E H
R L E C T U R E R R R E
O A        T N R R E A
R P        N O O P C D
E I        R L R D O M
N C        L O E C A I
I N R L I E F A T E C S
A I T S S E N O C A H T
R R I N S T R U C T O R
T P U S T E A C H E R E
I O O R W O L L E F D S
C R R G O V E R N E S S
```

COACH	GOVERNESS	PROFESSOR
COUNSELLOR	HEADMASTER	TEACHER
DEAN	HEADMISTRESS	TRAINER
DOCTOR	INSTRUCTOR	TUTOR
DON	LECTURER	
FELLOW	PRINCIPAL	

Puzzle 45: Fish For Dinner

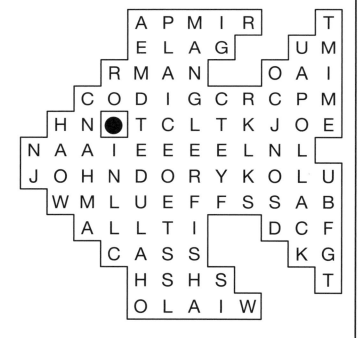

```
    A P M I R         T
    E L A G         U M
    R M A N       O A I
    C O D I G C R C P M
  H N ● T C L T K J O E
N A A I E E E E L N L
J O H N D O R Y K O L U
W M L U E F F S S A B
  A L L T I       D C F
  C A S S         K G T
    H S H S
    O L A I W
```

ANGLER FISH	MONKFISH	SOLE
BASS	PERCH	TROUT
COD	PLAICE	TUNA
JOHN DORY	POLLACK	WHITING
MACKEREL	SALMON	

Puzzle 46: Languages In Europe

```
A N A I C I L A G I H N
P N A I N I A R K U N N
O O L I T H U A N I A N
E T R I N S R G N I I A
N H N T S I A I N A N I
A G S I U R D A N L O G
I H A I I G B R L E T E
T N A A N L U G A U S W
A R N T A R R E R S E R
O S F A E R O E S E A O
R N A L A T A C N E E N
C I D N A L E C I D R K
```

ALBANIAN	GALICIAN	PORTUGUESE
CATALAN	GREEK	RUSSIAN
CORNISH	HUNGARIAN	SARDINIAN
CROATIAN	ICELANDIC	UKRAINIAN
ESTONIAN	LITHUANIAN	
FAEROESE	NORWEGIAN	

Puzzle 47: Gamers' Corner

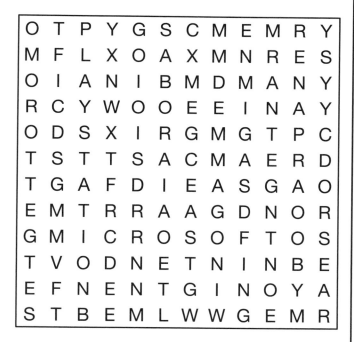

```
O T P Y G S C M E M R Y
M F L X O A X M N R E S
O I A N I B M D M A N Y
R C Y W O O E E I N A Y
O D S X I R G M G T P C
T S T T S A C M A E R D
T G A F D I E A S G A O
E M T R R A A G D N O R
G M I C R O S O F T O S
T V O D N E T N I N B E
E F N E N T G I N O Y A
S T B E M L W W G E M R
```

DREAMCAST	MEGADRIVE	PLAYSTATION
DSI	MICROSOFT	SONY
GAME BOY	NES	WII
GAME GEAR	NINTENDO	XBOX

Puzzle 48: Plug-In Equipment

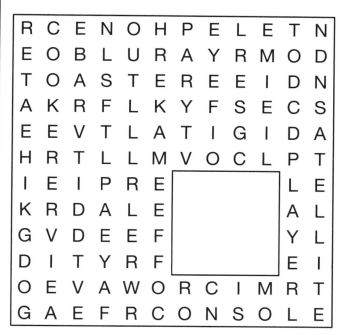

```
R C E N O H P E L E T N
E O B L U R A Y R M O D
T O A S T E R E E I D N
A K R F L K Y F S E C S
E E V T L A T I G I D A
H R T L L M V O C L P T
I E I P R E       L E
K R D A L E       A L
G V D E E F       Y L
D I T Y R F       E I
O E V A W O R C I M R T
G A E F R C O N S O L E
```

BLU-RAY	DIGITAL TV	RADIO
CD PLAYER	DVD PLAYER	SATELLITE
COFFEE	GRILL	TELEPHONE
MAKER	HEATER	TELEVISION
CONSOLE	KETTLE	TOASTER
COOKER	MICROWAVE	

Puzzle 49: Feeling Sleepy

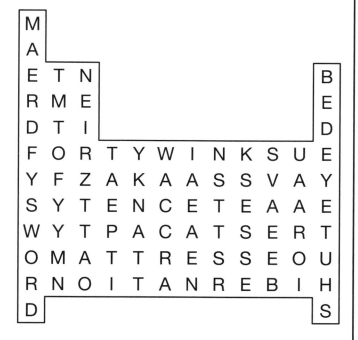

```
M
A
E T N             B
R M E             E
D T I             D
F O R T Y W I N K S U E
Y F Z A K A A S S V A Y
S Y T E N C E T E A A E
W Y T P A C A T S E R T
O M A T T R E S S E O U
R N O I T A N R E B I H
D                   S
```

BED	FORTY WINKS	SACK TIME
DOZE	HIBERNATION	SHUT EYE
DREAM	MATTRESS	SIESTA
DROWSY	NAP	TRANCE
DUVET	REST	

Puzzle 50: Musical Instruments

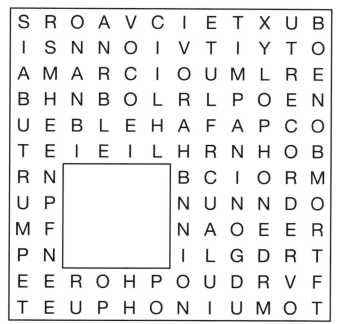

```
S R O A V C I E T X U B
I S N N O I V T I Y T O
A M A R C I O U M L R E
B H N B O L R L P O E N
U E B L E H A F A P C O
T E I E I L H R N H O B
R N       B C I O R M
U P       N U N N D O
M F       N A O E E R
P N       I L G D R T
E E R O H P O U D R V F
T E U P H O N I U M O T
```

CLARINET	ORGAN	TUBA
CORNET	PIANO	VIOLA
DOUBLE BASS	RECORDER	VIOLIN
EUPHONIUM	TIMPANI	XYLOPHONE
FLUTE	TROMBONE	
FRENCH HORN	TRUMPET	

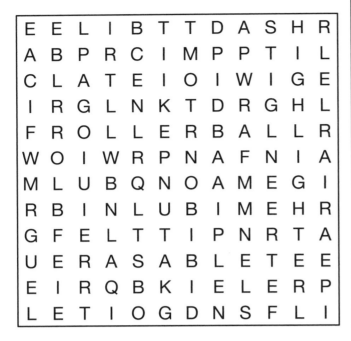

Puzzle 51: Types Of Pen

```
E E L I B T T D A S H R
A B P R C I M P P T I L
C L A T E I O I W I G E
I R G L N K T D R G H L
F R O L L E R B A L L R
W O I W R P N A F N I A
M L U B Q N O A M E G I
R B I N L U B I M E H R
G F E L T T I P N R T A
U E R A S A B L E T E E
E I R Q B K I E L E R P
L E T I O G D N S F L I
```

BALLPOINT   FIBRE TIP   REED
CROW QUILL   FOUNTAIN   ROLLER BALL
DIP   HIGHLIGHTER
ERASABLE   MARKER
FELT TIP   PERMANENT

Puzzle 52: Gemstones

```
        Y I Z O R E
        B E L T O P A Z
      U E Y E R E G I T O
      R I L U Z A L S I P A L
      C E N I R U T N E V A K
      O B L L Q A O Z P U
        R M R E U C O N
          A A S P R Z
            L O S I
            V R T Z
              E Z
              L L
```

AMBER   LAPIS LAZULI   RUBY
AVENTURINE   OPAL   TIGEREYE
CORAL   PEARL   TOPAZ
KUNZITE   ROSE QUARTZ   ZIRCON

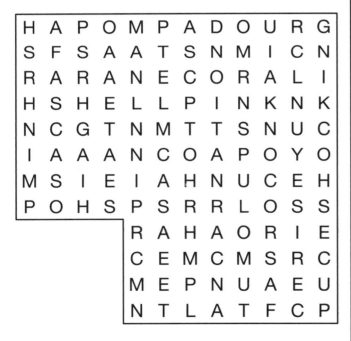

Puzzle 53: Shades Of Pink

```
H A P O M P A D O U R G
S F S A A T S N M I C N
R A R A N E C O R A L I
H S H E L L P I N K N K
N C G T N M T T S N U C
I A A A N C O A P O Y O
M S I E I A H N U C E H
P O H S P S R R L O S S
      R A H A O R I E
      C E M C M S R C
      M E P N U A E U
      N T L A T F C P
```

AMARANTH   FUCHSIA   PUCE
CARNATION   HOT   SALMON
CERISE   MAGENTA   SHELL PINK
CORAL   PEACH   SHOCKING
CYCLAMEN   PERSIAN
FRENCH ROSE   POMPADOUR

Puzzle 54: Types Of Plant

```
N P B U R H S U B R L N
A I G N D N S U C A S E
D I E N S E O U T E I F
O S G V N E M B G C T L
R L N P E R E N N I A L
C N E L G G R D I C B C
R N C U N R E F L L F T
A C F B W E A T P I C E
S G N E R V I S A M N P
L B G T G E I T S B N G
V E V R F L H N E E L T
V D I E F L O W E R R E
```

BUSH   GRASS   SHRUB
CACTUS   HERB   TREE
CLIMBER   MOSS   VEGETABLE
EVERGREEN   PERENNIAL   VINE
FERN   SAPLING
FLOWER   SEEDLING

Puzzle 55: Famous Queens

```
V A V I C T O R I A T R
V L S L O O Y A N I L R
E N I L O R A C A N H V
G N T A A B R R C A T F
H U O M E I T T C T E L
L N I H C A E A I I B I
U E S N P L H E D T A E
L C B O E E C A U B Z U
O E E A L V S B O R I A
B L N E S P E R B I L N
C O N I T I T R E F E N
R V E P O L E N E P N E
```

ANNE
BOUDICCA
CAROLINE
CLEOPATRA
ELEANOR
ELIZABETH

GUINEVERE
HELEN
ISABEL
MARY
NEFERTITI
PENELOPE

PERSEPHONE
SHEBA
TITANIA
VICTORIA

Puzzle 56: Jackets, Coats And More

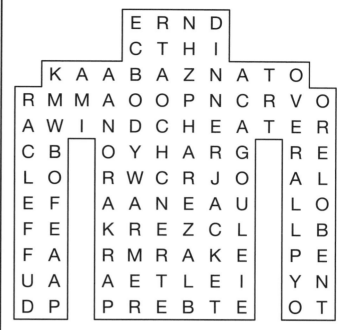

```
          E R N D
          C T H I
    K A A B A Z N A T O
R M M A O O P N C R V O
A W I N D C H E A T E R
C B   O Y H A R G   R E
L O   R W C R J O   A L
E F   A A N E A U   L B
F E   K R E Z C L   P E
F A   R M R A K E   Y N
U A   A E T L E I   O T
D P   P R E B T E   O T
```

ANORAK
BLAZER
BODY-WARMER
BOLERO
CAGOULE

CAPE
DINNER
JACKET
DUFFEL
MAC
OVERALL

PARKA
RAIN
TRENCH COAT
WINDCHEATER

Puzzle 57: Entertaining Events

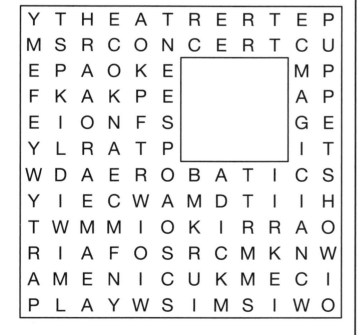

```
Y T H E A T R E R T E P
M S R C O N C E R T C U
E P A O K E         M P
F K A K P E         A P
E I O N F S         G E
Y L R A T P         I T
W D A E R O B A T I C S
Y I E C W A M D T I I H
T W M M I O K I R R A O
R I A F O S R C M K N W
A M E N I C U K M E C I
P L A Y W S I M S I W O
```

AEROBATICS
CINEMA
CIRCUS
COMEDY
FAIR
FIREWORKS

KARAOKE
MAGICIAN
MUSICAL
PANTOMIME
PARTY
PLAY

PUPPET
SHOW
SPORT
THEATRE

Puzzle 58: Pets In A Pickle

```
I T O R R A P R I P A E
T R P Y E C A T K C U D
P I A H E T H E M R B R
D G M G S K S I D I U A
P U L O R I N M C O D Z
U A I A O T F O A K G I
P N B T H T L D E H E L
P A R A K E E T L G R N
Y O E P O N Y B E O I S
T C G I P A E N I U G P
P C H I N C H I L L A U
F E R R E T I B B A R D
```

BUDGERIGAR
CAT
CHICKEN
CHINCHILLA
DOG
DUCK
FERRET
GERBIL

GOAT
GOLDFISH
GUINEA PIG
HAMSTER
HORSE
IGUANA
KITTEN
LIZARD

PARAKEET
PARROT
PIGEON
PONY
PUPPY
RABBIT
RAT
TORTOISE

Puzzle 59: London Train Stations

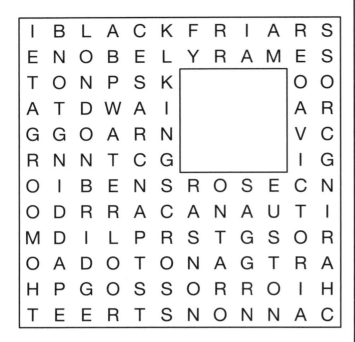

```
I B L A C K F R I A R S
E N O B E L Y R A M E S
T O N P S K       O O
A T D W A I       A R
G G O A R N       V C
R N N T C G       I G
O I B E N S R O S E C N
O D R R A C A N A U T I
M D I L P R S T G S O R
O A D O T O N A G T R A
H P G O S S O R R O I H
T E E R T S N O N N A C
```

BLACKFRIARS   MARYLEBONE
CANNON STREET   MOORGATE
CHARING CROSS   PADDINGTON
EUSTON   ST PANCRAS
KING'S CROSS   VICTORIA
LONDON BRIDGE   WATERLOO

Puzzle 60: Shapes Go Ape

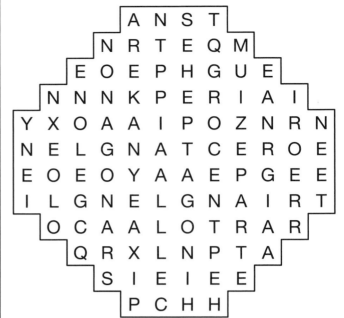

```
      A N S T
      N R T E Q M
    E O E P H G U E
    N N N K P E R I A I
  Y X O A A I P O Z N R N
  N E L G N A T C E R O E
  E O E O Y A A E P G E E
  I L G N E L G N A I R T
  O C A A L O T R A R
    Q R X L N P T A
      S I E I E E
      P C H H
```

CIRCLE   NONAGON   TRAPEZIUM
HEART   PENTAGON   TRIANGLE
HEPTAGON   POLYGON
HEXAGON   RECTANGLE
KITE   SQUARE

Puzzle 61: Relatively Speaking

```
O D D U B H E N R E E E
W A L N I R E H T O M D
D A N I S U O C L U N A
U N L S A U N T M M N G
G R A N D M O T H E R U
I G L B I A S S P E I R
N U E H S R U H E D R S
U E L C N U E G A D I U
      E W H H H S R G
      M I R P T T R L
      R F N E O A E T
      A E R E E L F R
```

AUNT   MOTHER-IN-LAW
BROTHER   MUM
COUSIN   NEPHEW
DAD   NIECE
DAUGHTER   SISTER
FATHER-IN-LAW   SON
GRANDMOTHER   UNCLE
HUSBAND   WIFE

Puzzle 62: Reptiles Roundup

```
C O I N D L C A I M A N
R L K N I K S T C T O A
O N A Z U P O H R G K S
C R A I C R A O A O C D
O R O O T M T R A E E A
D O U O E A D N R E G R
I R I L G O A Y N E S I
L S E I D U N D A L T G
E O L O G T N E U T G G
N L M I S K L V I R L O
A O A I O A L I R U O D
K N E K A N S L L T U I
```

ALLIGATOR   LIZARD
CAIMAN   SKINK
CHAMELEON   SNAKE
CROCODILE   TERRAPIN
GECKO   THORNY DEVIL
IGUANA   TORTOISE
KOMODO DRAGON   TURTLE

Puzzle 63: Sports To Try

```
A  S  U  S  F  E  K  Y  J  U  D  O
A  E  G  I  H  O  T  T  B  N  R  L
S  I  A  N  R  A  O  A  E  G  L  E
H  O  I  N  I  I  N  T  R  A  U  B
S  O  B  E  C  L  B  D  B  A  G  R
A  C  I  T  S  A  C  T  B  A  K  M
U  R  V  O  L  L  E  Y  B  A  L  L
Q  I  D  L  E  K  C  G  C  N  L  L
S  C  I  T  S  A  N  M  Y  G  L  L
B  K  B  A  D  M  I  N  T  O  N  M
H  E  B  C  Q  R  U  N  N  I  N  G
S  T  S  U  H  O  C  K  E  Y  C  I
```

BADMINTON
BASKETBALL
CRICKET
CYCLING
FOOTBALL
GYMNASTICS

HANDBALL
HOCKEY
JUDO
KARATE
NETBALL
RUGBY

RUNNING
SQUASH
TENNIS
VOLLEYBALL

Puzzle 64: Flower Power

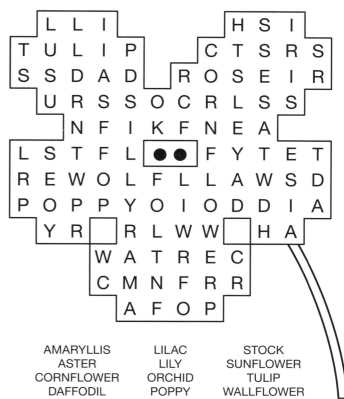

```
      L  L  I           H  S  I
   T  U  L  I  P        C  T  S  R  S
   S  S  D  A  D     R  O  S  E  I  R
      U  R  S  S  O  C  R  L  S  S
         N  F  I  K  F  N  E  A
   L  S  T  F  L  ● ● F  Y  T  E  T
   R  E  W  O  L  F  L  L  A  W  S  D
   P  O  P  P  Y  O  I  O  D  D  I  A
   Y  R     R  L  W  W     H  A
      W  A  T  R  E  C
      C  M  N  F  R  R
         A  F  O  P
```

AMARYLLIS
ASTER
CORNFLOWER
DAFFODIL
IRIS

LILAC
LILY
ORCHID
POPPY
ROSE

STOCK
SUNFLOWER
TULIP
WALLFLOWER

Puzzle 65: Roast Dinner

```
E  R  E  W  O  L  F  I  L  U  A  C
N  O  M  M  A  G  E  L  P  A  C  U
E  A              E  O  A  H  M  N
O  S              B  C  I  M  C  B
A  T              K  C  T  R  S  R
K  P              K  O  G  C  P  O
R  O  R  M  Y  E  G  R  R  A  R  P
N  T  E  P  N  E  A  B  R  R  O  N
M  A  R  K  D  V  K  S  A  R  U  N
A  T  E  E  Y  K  N  R  K  O  T  W
P  O  W  G  N  I  F  F  U  T  S  S
E  S  A  E  P  G  O  N  H  T  U  O
```

BEEF
BROCCOLI
CARROT
CAULIFLOWER
CHICKEN
GAMMON

GRAVY
LAMB
PARSNIP
PEAS
PORK
ROAST

POTATO
SPROUTS
STUFFING
SWEDE
TURKEY

Puzzle 66: London Underground Lines

```
H  N  O  R  T  H  E  R  N  L  T  E
L  A  R  T  N  E  C  A  T  E  E  C
P  T  M  L  R  T             I  I
J  I  A  M  C  E             A  H
O  L  C  T  E  E             L  A
N  O  C  C  J  R             T  I
E  P  L  I  A  U  S  T  V  A  I  R
L  O  C  R  R  D  B  M  U  L  O  O
E  R  E  T  E  C  I  I  I  C  M  T
B  T  E  S  L  K  L  L  L  T  S  C
E  E  N  I  M  M  A  E  L  E  H  I
S  M  B  D  S  Y  O  B  I  Y  E  V
```

BAKERLOO
CENTRAL
CIRCLE
DISTRICT
HAMMERSMITH

JUBILEE
METROPOLITAN
NORTHERN
PICCADILLY
VICTORIA

Puzzle 67: Types Of Book

```
I N G U I D E B O O K S
S O H N F E C N A M O R
O N I C I I A E C B E T
C F S N C F M H I F E R
L I T C S I I O E X E A
A C O S R L G R T L E E
S T R C D R E B L A F N
S I Y R A N O I T C I D
I O E P C O R L
C N H E K H A T
S Y R E T S Y M
H F A N T A S Y
```

ATLAS
BIOGRAPHY
CHILDREN'S
CLASSICS
CRIME
DICTIONARY

FANTASY
GUIDEBOOK
HISTORY
MYSTERY
NON FICTION
REFERENCE

ROMANCE
SCI-FI
TEXTBOOK
THRILLER

Puzzle 68: Animal Safari

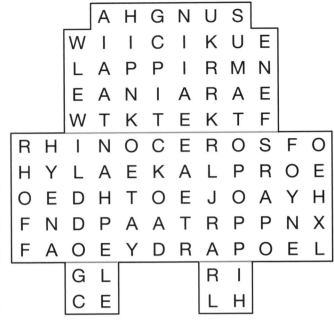

```
        A H G N U S
      W I I C I K U E
      L A P P I R M N
      E A N I A R A E
      W T K T E K T F
R H I N O C E R O S F O
H Y L A E K A L P R O E
O E D H T O E J O A Y H
F N D P A A T R P P N X
F A O E Y D R A P O E L
    G L           R I
    C E           L H
```

ANTELOPE
ELEPHANT
HIPPOPOTAMUS
HYENA
GIRAFFE
GNU
JACKAL

LEOPARD
LION
OKAPI
ORYX
OSTRICH
RHINOCEROS
WILD DOG

Puzzle 69: Football Clubs

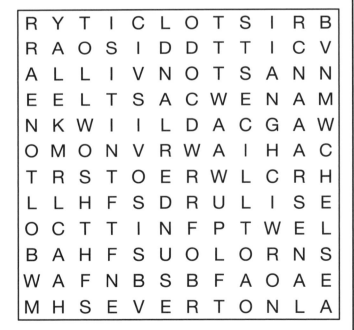

```
R Y T I C L O T S I R B
R A O S I D D T T I C V
A L L I V N O T S A N N
E E L T S A C W E N A M
N K W I I L D A C G A W
O M O N V R W A I H A C
T R S T O E R W L C R H
L L H F S D R U L I S E
O C T T I N F P T W E L
B A H F S U O L O R N S
W A F N B S B F A O A E
M H S E V E R T O N L A
```

ARSENAL
ASTON VILLA
BOLTON
BRISTOL CITY
CARDIFF
CHELSEA

EVERTON
FULHAM
LIVERPOOL
NEWCASTLE
NORWICH
STOKE

SUNDERLAND
WATFORD
WEST HAM
WIGAN

Puzzle 70: UK Prime Ministers

```
G M A C D O N A L D C G
C D A S Q U I T H N A L
T H O C H U R C H I L L
R B A U M E D E N W L O
I E A M G I A T R D A Y
A C H L B L L T H L G D
L C A C F E A L H A H G
B T E T T O R S A B A E
      T A U L H N N O
      C L H R A O D R
      B L E T A I M G
      C A M E R O N E
```

ASQUITH
ATTLEE
BALDWIN
BALFOUR
BLAIR
CALLAGHAN
CAMERON
CHAMBERLAIN

CHURCHILL
DOUGLAS-HOME
EDEN
HEATH
LLOYD GEORGE
MACDONALD
MACMILLAN
THATCHER

Puzzle 71: Gone Camping

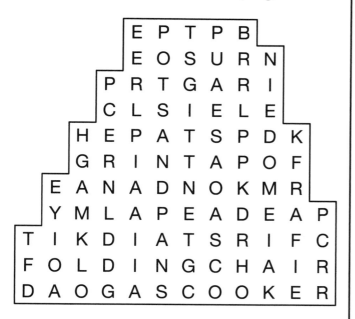

```
        E P T P B
      E O S U R N
    P R T G A R I
    C L S I E L E
    H E P A T S P D K
    G R I N T A P O F
  E A N A D N O K M R
  Y M L A P E A D E A P
T I K D I A T S R I F C
F O L D I N G C H A I R
D A O G A S C O O K E R
```

BUG SPRAY   GAS COOKER   ROPE
CAMP SITE   LANTERN   STAKE
FIRST-AID KIT   PEG   TENT
FOLDING   POTS AND   TORCH
CHAIR   PANS

Puzzle 72: Clothing Conundrum

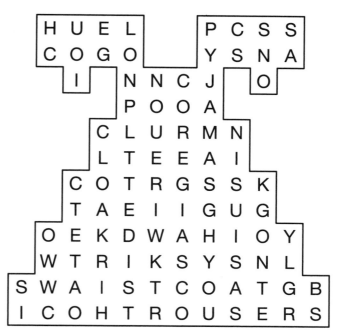

```
H U E L           P C S S
C O G O           Y S N A
    I       N N C J     O
            P O O A
        C L U R M N
        L T E E A I
        C O T R G S S K
        T A E I I G U G
      O E K D W A H I O Y
      W T R I K S Y S N L
    S W A I S T C O A T G B
    I C O H T R O U S E R S
```

BLOUSE   LEGGINGS   SWEATER
CARDIGAN   PYJAMAS   TROUSERS
CLOAK   SARONG   T-SHIRT
KIMONO   SKIRT   WAISTCOAT

Puzzle 73: All Amphibians

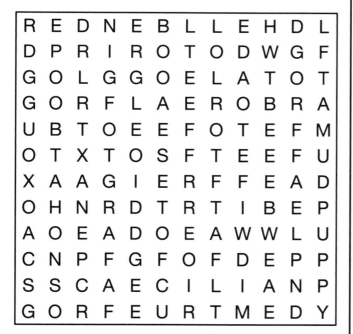

```
R E D N E B L L E H D L
D P R I R O T O D W G F
G O L G G O E L A T O T
G O R F L A E R O B R A
U B T O E E F O T E F M
O T X T O S F T E E F U
X A A G I E R F F E A D
O H N R D T R T I B E P
A O E A D O E A W W L U
C N P F G F O F D E P P
S S C A E C I L I A N P
G O R F E U R T M E D Y
```

ARBOREAL FROG   MUD PUPPY
AXOLOTL   NEWT
CAECILIAN   OLM
CONGO EEL   SPADEFOOT
DWARF SIREN   TREE FROG
HELLBENDER   TRUE FROG
LEAF FROG
MIDWIFE TOAD

Puzzle 74: Dogs, Dogs, Dogs

```
N D N U O H Y E R G M R
N P O I N T E R F O D H
A F G H A N H O U N D R
I B N L E U X N U N O E
T O R U O H T O U T B V
A X A M O A H O T S E E
M E P U I N H W A E R I
L R N N A D E L T I M R
A D D Z O I U U D L A T
D O I O L K P H C L N E
G B L E I N A P S O H R
I B R E Z U A N H C S I
```

AFGHAN HOUND   IBIZAN HOUND
BLOODHOUND   MOUNTAIN DOG
BOXER   POINTER
COLLIE   RETRIEVER
DALMATIAN   ROTTWEILER
DOBERMAN   SALUKI
FOXHOUND   SCHNAUZER
GREYHOUND   SPANIEL

Puzzle 75: Brass Instruments

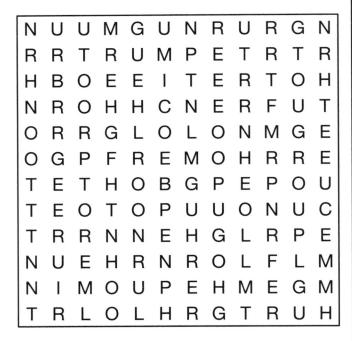

```
N U U M G U N R U R G N
R R T R U M P E T R T R
H B O E E I T E R T O H
N R O H H C N E R F U T
O R R G L O L O N M G E
O G P F R E M O H R R E
T E T H O B G P E P O U
T E O T O P U U O N U C
T R R N N E H G L R P E
N U E H R N R O L F L M
N I M O U P E H M E G M
T R L O L H R G T R U H
```

BUGLE	FRENCH HORN
CORNET	TENOR HORN
EUPHONIUM	TROMBONE
FLUGELHORN	TRUMPET

Puzzle 76: Magic Tricks

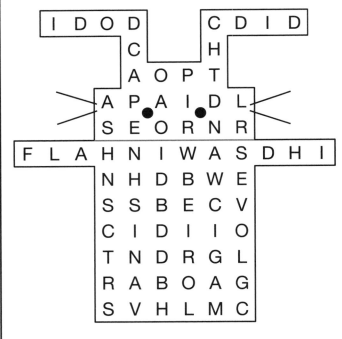

```
        I D O D        C D I D
            C              H
            A              O P T
          A P A I D L
          S E O R N R
    F L A H N I W A S D H I
            N H D B W E
            S S B E C V
            C I D I I O
            T N D R G L
            R A B O A G
            S V H L M C
```

CAPE	HAT
CARDS	MAGIC WAND
COINS	RABBIT
DICE	SAW IN HALF
GLOVES	VANISH

Puzzle 77: In The Kitchen

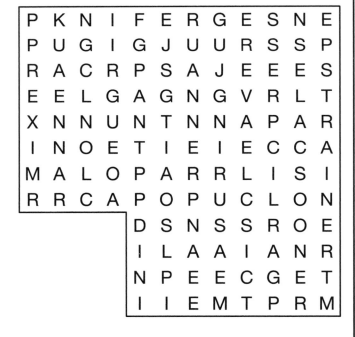

```
P K N I F E R G E S N E
P U G I G J U U R S S P
R A C R P S A J E E E S
E E L G A G N G V R L T
X N N U N T N N A P A R
I N O E T I E I E C C A
M A L O P A R R L I S I
R R C A P O P U C L O N
      D S N S S R O E
        I L A A I A N R
        N P E E C G E T
        I I E M T P R M
```

CAN OPENER	MEASURING JUG
CLEAVER	MIXER
GARLIC PRESS	ROLLING PIN
GRATER	SCALES
KNIFE	SPATULA
LADLE	STRAINER
MEASURING CUP	TEASPOON

Puzzle 78: Playing Music

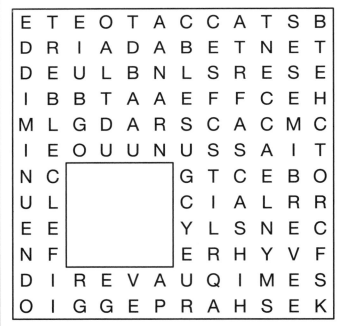

```
E T E O T A C C A T S B
D R I A D A B E T N E T
D E U L B N L S R E S E
I B B T A A E F F C E H
M L G D A R S C A C M C
I E O U U N U S S A I T
N C         G T C E B O
U L         C I A L R R
E E         Y L S N E C
N F         E R H Y V F
D I R E V A U Q I M E S
O I G G E P R A H S E K
```

ACCENT	KEY SIGNATURE
ARPEGGIO	NATURAL
BASS CLEF	REST
CODA	SEMIBREVE
CRESCENDO	SEMIQUAVER
CROTCHET	SHARP
DIMINUENDO	STACCATO
FLAT	TREBLE CLEF

Puzzle 79: In The Bathroom

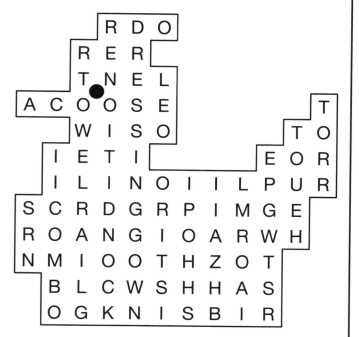

		R	D	O			
	R	E	R				
	T	N	E	L			
A	C	O	O	S	E		T
	W	I	S	O		T	O
I	E	T	I		E	O	R
I	L	I	N	O	I	L	P	U	R
S	C	R	D	G	R	P	I	M	G	E
R	O	A	N	G	I	O	A	R	W	H
N	M	I	O	O	T	H	Z	O	T
B	L	C	W	S	H	H	A	S
O	G	K	N	I	S	B	I	R

BATH   SHAMPOO
COMB   SHOWER
CONDITIONER   SINK
DRESSING GOWN   SOAP
RAZOR   TOILET
RUG   TOWEL RAIL

Puzzle 80: Olympic Cities

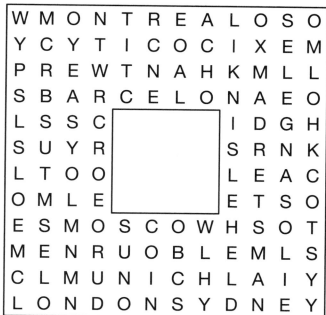

W	M	O	N	T	R	E	A	L	O	S	O
Y	C	Y	T	I	C	O	C	I	X	E	M
P	R	E	W	T	N	A	H	K	M	L	L
S	B	A	R	C	E	L	O	N	A	E	O
L	S	S	C					I	D	G	H
S	U	Y	R					S	R	N	K
L	T	O	O					L	E	A	C
O	M	L	E					E	T	S	O
E	S	M	O	S	C	O	W	H	S	O	T
M	E	N	R	U	O	B	L	E	M	L	S
C	L	M	U	N	I	C	H	L	A	I	Y
L	O	N	D	O	N	S	Y	D	N	E	Y

AMSTERDAM   MELBOURNE   SEOUL
ANTWERP   MEXICO CITY   ST LOUIS
BARCELONA   MONTREAL   STOCKHOLM
HELSINKI   MOSCOW   SYDNEY
LONDON   MUNICH
LOS ANGELES   ROME

Puzzle 81: Train Ride

R	R	O	A	R	E	T	U	R	N	K	S
N	O	I	T	A	L	L	E	C	N	A	C
O	R	G	U	A	R	D	R	I	V	E	R
I	N	T	E	R	C	I	T	Y	A	P	T
T	S	S	A	L	C	T	S	R	I	F	A
A	I	S	S	E	R	P	X	E	I	F	N
N	N	C	C	L	I				O	O
I	G	I	K	R	D				R	I
T	L	A	T	E	L				E	T
S	E	Y	L	T	T				P	A
E	A	A	S	T	L	O	C	A	L	U	T
D	Y	S	E	A	S	O	N	P	A	S	S

CANCELLATION   INTERCITY
DAY TRIP   LOCAL
DELAY   RETURN
DESTINATION   SEASON PASS
DRIVER   SINGLE
EXPRESS   STATION
FIRST CLASS   SUPER OFF-PEAK
GUARD   TICKET

Puzzle 82: Types Of Trees

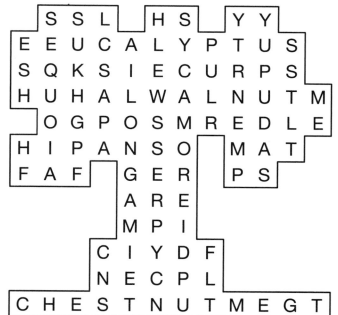

	S	S	L		H	S		Y	Y
E	E	U	C	A	L	Y	P	T	U	S
S	Q	K	S	I	E	C	U	R	P	S
H	U	H	A	L	W	A	L	N	U	T	M
	O	G	P	O	S	M	R	E	D	L	E
H	I	P	A	N	S	O		M	A	T
F	A	F		G	E	R		P	S
				A	R	E
				M	P	I
			C	I	Y	D	F
			N	E	C	P	L
C	H	E	S	T	N	U	T	M	E	G	T

APPLE   FIG   SEQUOIA
ASH   FIR   SPRUCE
CHESTNUT   MAGNOLIA   SYCAMORE
CYPRESS   OAK   WALNUT
ELDER   PALM
EUCALYPTUS   PINE

Puzzle 83: Opposites

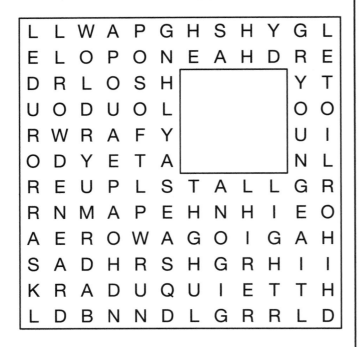

L	L	W	A	P	G	H	S	H	Y	G	L
E	L	O	P	O	N	E	A	H	D	R	E
D	R	L	O	S	H				Y	T
U	O	D	U	O	L			O	O
R	W	R	A	F	Y			U	I
O	D	Y	E	T	A			N	L
R	E	U	P	L	S	T	A	L	L	G	R
R	N	M	A	P	E	H	N	H	I	E	O
A	E	R	O	W	A	G	O	I	G	A	H
S	A	D	H	R	S	H	G	R	H	I	I
K	R	A	D	U	Q	U	I	E	T	T	H
L	D	B	N	N	D	L	G	R	R	L	D

BAD	FULL	HARD	OLD
GOOD	FAR	SOFT	SHORT
DARK	NEAR	HIGH	TALL
LIGHT	FAT	LOW	
DRY	THIN	LOUD	
WET	HAPPY	YOUNG	
EMPTY	SAD	QUIET	

Puzzle 84: Pantomime Characters

A	F	G	E	D	B	P	D
S	L	L	O	T	I	L	A
S	R	A	O	L	I	B	M
N	K	E	D	W	D	H	E
O	S	S	T	D	D	I	W	A	E	D	C
W	G	R	E	S	I	A	L	W	U	U	E
Q	P	U	S	S	I	N	B	O	O	T	S
U	B	N	D	J	U	S	K	G	C	N	Y
E	N	C	S	O	U	B	Y	C	I	K	S
E	D	S	A	B	A	B	I	L	A	B	S
N	A	P	R	E	T	E	P	U	G	J	S
A	L	L	E	R	E	D	N	I	C	U	A

ALADDIN	GOLDILOCKS	SNOW QUEEN
ALI BABA	JACK	SNOW WHITE
BEAUTY	NURSE	UGLY SISTERS
BIG BAD WOLF	PETER PAN	
CINDERELLA	PUSS IN	
DAME	BOOTS	

Puzzle 85: Easter Time

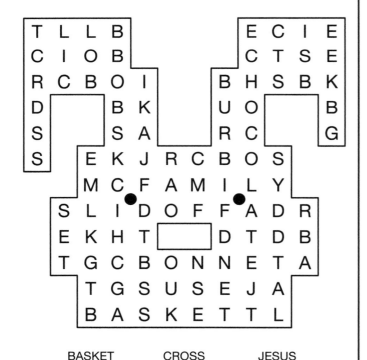

BASKET	CROSS	JESUS
BONNET	DAFFODILS	RABBIT
CHICKS	EGGS	SUNDAY
CHOCOLATE	FAMILY	TOMB

Puzzle 86: Everything's Yellow

G	E	C	U	S	T	A	R	D	S	S	T
F	L	I	H	K	E	L	A	B	R	Y	E
A	U	A	T	C	E	F	U	E	E	G	N
O	T	B	E	M	F	T	W	E	G	B	C
T	O	G	O	O	T	O	N	Y	G	H	A
D	A	N	D	E	L	I	O	N	I	U	N
I	S	I	R	F	R	L	U	C	D	R	A
L	L	C	N	A	K	S	K	E	I	I	R
P	U	U	G	S	E	S	E	E	H	C	Y
P	S	R	A	H	R	Y	O	L	M	E	I
A	A	M	T	O	C	N	L	N	Y	R	N
M	F	M	U	S	T	A	R	D	T	R	R

BUTTERCUP	DAFFODIL	MARGARINE
CANARY	DANDELION	MUSTARD
CHEESE	DIGGERS	SUNFLOWERS
CHICKS	EGG YOLK	THE SUN
CUSTARD	LEMONS	

Puzzle 87: On The Move

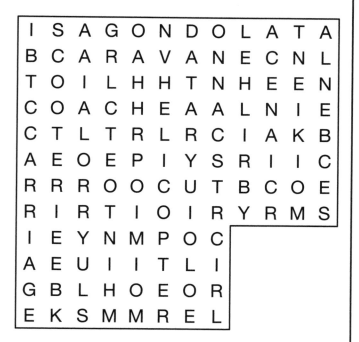

```
I S A G O N D O L A T A
B C A R A V A N E C N L
T O I L H H T N H E E N
C O A C H E A A L N I E
C T L T R L R C I A K B
A E O E P I Y S R I I C
R R R O O C U T B C O E
R I R T I O I R Y R M S
I E Y N M P O C
A E U I I T L I
G B L H O E O R
E K S M M R E L
```

AEROPLANE   COACH   SCOOTER
BICYCLE   GONDOLA   SHIP
BOAT   HELICOPTER   TRAIN
CARAVAN   LIMOUSINE   UNICYCLE
CARRIAGE   LORRY
CHARIOT   MOTORBIKE

Puzzle 88: Edible Berries

```
S L L B B E C R S S G B
Y E E L L B B B R T R L E
G R R R A R E R A U B A
L O R T C R A S E R Y C
D R O E K W P B O R R Y
E B R S B B E E R A R C
R Y C E E R R Y N R E S
Y R R R B E B S B B S
L R R Y R A E D A B L R
Y Y B A Y R R R L L I R
R C Y E R R P A R E B Y
R B Y Y B E A E Y Y Y P
```

BILBERRY   ELDERBERRY
BLACKBERRY   GOOSEBERRY
BLUEBERRY   RASPBERRY
CRANBERRY   STRAWBERRY

Puzzle 89: Types Of Shoe

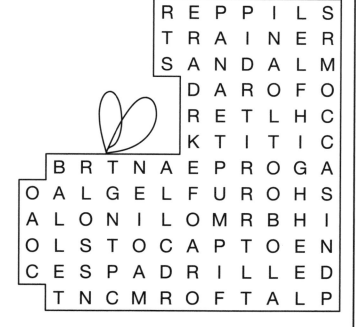

```
        R E P P   I L S
        T R A I N E R R
        S A N D A L M
        D A R O F O
        R E T L H C
        K T I T I C
B R T N A E P R O G A
O A L G E L F U R O H S
A L O N I L O M R B H I
O L S T O C A P T O E N
C E S P A D R I L L E D
T N C M R O F T A L P
```

BALLET   FLIP-FLOP   SLIPPER
BOOT   HIGH HEEL   SNEAKER
CAP TOE   MOCCASIN   STILETTO
CLOG   PLATFORM   TRAINER
COURT   PUMP
ESPADRILLE   SANDAL

Puzzle 90: Feeling Great

```
R V B U F Y N K I R P K
Y I L A U G H I N G A N
I P A G L P          R I
W O L N L J          M P
H O K U O R          G D
N K N Y F G          N E
I K O D B R N L L R I L
W U A F E H E I P D Z K
S G R L A R A E K H A C
P F N G N N F P H L M I
G N D R S D L U P C A T
P A N L L I V E L Y R W
```

AMAZING   LAUGHING
CHEERFUL   LIVELY
FULL OF BEANS   TICKLED PINK
HAPPY   WALKING ON AIR
JOYOUS   WONDERFUL

Puzzle 91: Orchestral Instruments

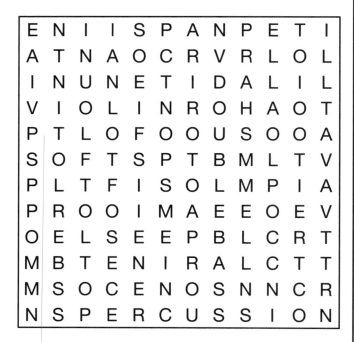

```
E N I I S P A N P E T I
A T N A O C R V R L O L
I N U N E T I D A L I L
V I O L I N R O H A O T
P T L O F O O U S O O A
S O F T S P T B M L T V
P L T F I S O L M P I A
P R O O I M A E E O E V
O E L S E E P B L C R T
M B T E N I R A L C T T
M S O C E N O S N N C R
N S P E R C U S S I O N
```

BASSOON
CELLO
CLARINET
DOUBLE BASS
FLUTE
HARP
HORN
OBOE
PERCUSSION
TIMPANI
TROMBONE
TRUMPET
VIOLA
VIOLIN

Puzzle 92: Burger Toppings

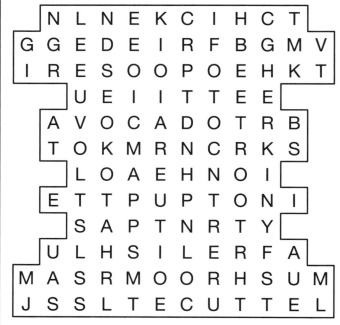

```
    N L N E K C I H C T
G G E D E I R F B G M V
I R E S O O P O E H K T
    U E I I T T E E
A V O C A D O T R B
T O K M R N C R K S
  L O A E H N O I
E T T P U P T O N I
  S A P T N R T Y
U L H S I L E R F A
M A S R M O O R H S U M
J S S L T E C U T T E L
```

AVOCADO
BEEF
BEETROOT
CHICKEN
FRIED EGG
GHERKIN
JALAPENO
KETCHUP
LETTUCE
MAYONNAISE
MINT
MUSHROOM
MUSTARD
PICKLE
RELISH
TOMATO

Puzzle 93: Board Games In The Box

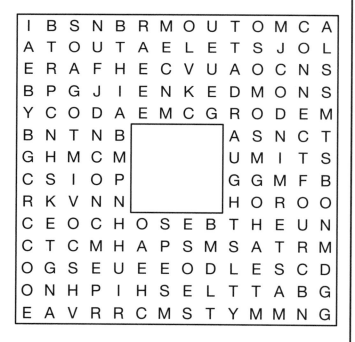

```
I B S N B R M O U T O M C A
A T O U T A E L E T S J O L
E R A F H E C V U A O C N S
B P G J I E N K E D M O N S
Y C O D A E M C G R O D E M
B N T N B       A S N C T
G H M C M       U M I T S
C S I O P       G G M F B
R K V N N       H O R O O
C E O C H O S E B T H E U N
C T C M H A P S M S A T R M
O G S E U E E O D L E S C D
O N H P I H S E L T T A B G
E A V R R C M S T Y M M N G
```

BACKGAMMON
BATTLESHIP
CHESS
CONNECT
FOUR
DRAUGHTS
LUDO
MAH-JONG
MASTERMIND
MONOPOLY
REVERSI

Puzzle 94: Capital Cities

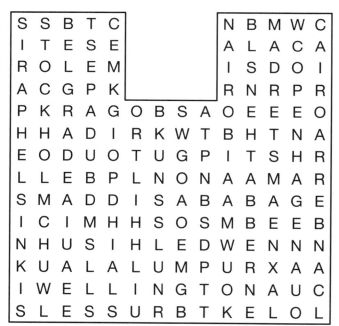

```
S S B T C         N B M W C
I T E S E         A L A C A
R O L E M         I S D O I
A C G P K         R N R P R
P K R A G O B S A O E E E O
H H A D I R K W T B H T N A
E O D U O T U G P I T S H R
L L E B P L N O N A A M A R
S M A D D I S A B A B A G E
I C I M H H S O S M B E E B
N H U S I H L E D W E N N N
K U A L A L U M P U R X A A
I W E L L I N G T O N A U C
S L E S S U R B T K E L O L
```

ADDIS ABABA
AMSTERDAM
ATHENS
BANGKOK
BELGRADE
BERNE
BRUSSELS
BUDAPEST
CAIRO
CANBERRA
COPENHAGEN
HELSINKI
KUALA LUMPUR
LIMA
LUXEMBOURG
NAIROBI
NEW DELHI
OSLO
PARIS
SANTIAGO
STOCKHOLM
WARSAW
WASHINGTON DC
WELLINGTON

Puzzle 95: Didn't Do My Homework

```
S N I A R T N O T F E L K T
W R E D O G A T E I T N W I
E E I M D O A A N I I I O K
R P Y O O N T N O S K O D O
I A H T D H E D N O O L N O
F P S P I L T I N K O N I T
T F R W O N D A D S T T W D
H O B T D E D S T T R E T N
G T S L P A O M O I E E U E
U U U P E D Y O L K T S O I
A O O N N B B I R B S F W R
C R A N O U T O F T I M E F
D I O O S F P T T F S W L L
B I K Y T Y A W A W E L B D
```

BLEW AWAY
BLEW OUT WINDOW
CAUGHT FIRE
COULDN'T DO IT
DOG ATE IT
DROPPED IN SINK
FRIEND TOOK IT
LEFT IT AT HOME

LEFT ON TRAIN
LOST MY BOOK
OUT OF PAPER
RAN OUT OF TIME
SISTER TOOK IT
SPILT INK ON IT
STOLEN
TOO BUSY

Puzzle 96: Breeds Of Cat

```
Y E S N L E T S Y E S C A B
B Y B Y A T S E M M I R Y B
T O R T O I S E S H E L L K
B N R M I T N I M B I A B M
E E T A N N A I S R E P N G
E S O I S M I B S T U X N B
Y P Y A E L R A B S N B P S
N Y G S S N E S I Y Y B N H
Y E E T T E B T H L E B C R
B X R M E O I P E E L B A I
S O T A M O S E B A H G Y E
E B S B A O A O C E B A I C
X N A M I O N K N A M A O A
K Y B I N U C M M O I R L T
```

ABYSSINIAN
BLACK
BOMBAY
BURMESE
MANX
PERSIAN

SIAMESE
SIBERIAN
SPHYNX
TABBY
TORTOISESHELL
TOYGER

Puzzle 97: Where Are You From?

```
G P N E A
A W H A S H S I K R U T
N R E S C E S E T L A M
A N N L I I N I J A I A
I G A U S T R A L I A N
T G R I T H T E P G C E
P M A E D S P O M A N Y
Y E F R E N C H C A J E
G         K I I S S R R
E
N
H
```

AMERICAN
AUSTRALIAN
EGYPTIAN
ENGLISH

FRENCH
GREEK
INDIAN
JAPANESE

MALTESE
SCOTTISH
TURKISH
WELSH

Puzzle 98: Putting On A Hat

```
L T T E R E B O
E L C L O D R B
T D A B Z E F R
A E T B R E A E
R K E B E R V C
I C M A O S I O
P O A D D T A W
S C E R R A T B
F F A I L L O O
E Z L P R K R Y
C O I B O W L E R R W R
R W Y T I T U R B A N T
```

AVIATOR
BASEBALL
BERET
BOWLER
CAP
COCKED

COWBOY
DEERSTALKER
FEDORA
FEZ
PIRATE
SOMBRERO

TOP
TRILBY
TURBAN
WIZARD'S

Cover the ice with penguins.

1 = black   2 = pink   3 = yellow

4 = orange   5 = brown   6 = grey

A feast fit for a king.

SUDOKU

The next section is full of Sudoku puzzles, a type of number puzzle that originated in Japan.

The overall aim is to fill in all the missing numbers in a grid. In a Sudoku grid, each row has nine squares, each column has nine squares, and each box has nine squares. When the puzzle is complete, every column, row and box must contain each of the numbers from 1 to 9, but only once.

In every Sudoku puzzle some of the numbers in the grid have been filled in already. You have to work out the numbers that go in each of the empty spaces.

The best way to start off solving a Sudoku puzzle is to look out forrows, columns and boxes which have lots of numbers already filled in, as these are often the easiest to complete. Then you're well on your way to completing the whole thing!

If you get completely stuck and can't work out which number goes where, don't panic – all of the answers are in the back of the book.

Puzzle: 1

9	5	1	2	7	6	8	4	3
3	8	4	9	5	1	2	7	6
6	7	2	8	4	3	5	1	9
1	3	9	7	6	8	4	2	5
2	4	8	3	1	5	6	4	7
5	6	7	4	9	2	1	3	8
4	9	3	1	8	7	6	5	2
8	2	6	5	3	4	7	9	1
7	1	5	6	2	9	3	8	4

Puzzle: 2

4	8	2		9		5	3	1
3	7	1	8	4	5	6	2	9
9	5	6	1	3	2	4	8	7
2		7	3		9	1	4	8
8		4		7		3		5
5		3	4		8	7		2
6	4	5	9	2	1	8	7	3
7	3	9	5	4	4	2	1	6
1	2	8		6		9	5	4

8		2				5		9
7	6	3	1	5		4	8	2
5	4	9		8	2	7	3	1
	3			1	4	6	5	
	9	4		2		3	1	
	5	8	7	3			9	
4	2	5	8	6		9	7	3
9	8	6		4	7	1	2	5
3		1				8		6

	9	7				4	8	
2	8	5		9		1	3	7
1	3	4	7		2	9	6	5
	5	8	2	6	3	7	4	
			9	4	8			
	6	3	1	5	7	8	2	
8	2	9	3		6	5	1	4
5	4	1		2		3	7	6
	7	6				2	9	

5	7	8				4	2	6
6	3	4	5		2	1	9	8
1		9				7		3
3	6	5		4		8	7	2
	8	2		5		9	3	
9	1	7		3		5	6	4
8		1				2		9
7	9	6	1		4	3	8	5
2	4	3				6	1	7

8	9		4	3			2	6
	2	4	9	5	6	8	1	3
	3	5	2	8	1	4	9	7
	7	6		9			4	1
				1				
9	1			4		3	7	
1	6	2	5	7	8	9	3	
3	5	9	1	2	4	7	6	
4	8			6	9		5	2

Puzzle: 7

2	3	9		1	4	7	5	6
1	4	8	7	6		9	2	3
5	7			3		8	1	
4	9			8	3			2
	2			5			9	
6			4	2			8	7
	1	2		9			4	5
3	8	5		4	6	1	7	9
9	6	4	5	7		2	3	8

Puzzle: 8

1	2	3	4		6	7	5	8
9	4	5	1	7	8	2	6	3
	6	7	2	3	5	4	1	
	9						8	
		8		5		1		
	7						2	
	5	2	8	4	9	6	3	
3	8	6	7	2	1	9	4	5
4	1	9	5		3	8	7	2

Puzzle: 9

5	3	4				1	6	9
9	7	2	1		3	5	8	4
1		8				2		3
4	1	5	6		7	3	9	8
		7		1		4		
6	9	3	4		8	7	2	1
7		6				8		2
3	8	9	2		1	6	4	5
2	5	1				9	3	7

Puzzle: 10

4	2	9						3
	7	5		2			9	
3	6	1		5	9	8	7	2
1	8		7	6	2	9	4	5
6	5	7		4		3	2	8
9	4	2	3	8	5		1	6
7	1	4	2	3		5	8	9
	9			7		1	3	
5						2	6	7

Puzzle: 11

8		5	3	2	7	1	4	6
		7	4					3
1		3		5		7	8	2
7	3	1	9	6		4	5	8
9		2		4		6		1
4	8	6		7	5	2	3	9
3	7	8		1		9		4
5					4	8		
2	1	4	7	9	8	3		5

Puzzle: 12

2	7	9	8	1	6	5		3
5	8	6		3	4	1	9	7
	4	1	7			6	2	8
6							1	5
8	3			7			6	2
1	2							9
7	1	8			3	2	5	
4	6	2	5	8		9	3	1
9		3	1	6	2	8	7	4

Puzzle: 13

2	7	9	1		5	3	8	6
	5	8				4	9	
3	4	6	9		2	7	5	1
	2		8	7	9		6	
7			6	2	4			8
	6		5	1	3		2	
9	8	2	7		1	6	4	3
	3	7				2	1	
4	1	5	2		6	8	7	9

Puzzle: 14

6		5		7		3		2
9	8	1	6		3	4	5	7
7	2	3	5	4	8	9	6	1
4		6				5		9
			2	9	7			
3		2				7		8
8	3	4	9	5	2	1	7	6
1	5	7	3		6	2	9	4
2		9		1		8		5

Puzzle: 15

9	5	3	6		8	4	7	2
6	8	2	4		7	5	3	1
	4	1	3	5	2	8	9	
	6			3			8	
			5	2	4			
	7			6			2	
	3	5	9	7	6	2	4	
8	2	6	1		3	9	5	7
4	9	7	2		5	6	1	3

Puzzle: 16

7		6	8	5	4	9		3
5	4	1	3	2		6	7	8
8	9	3	6	7	1	4		5
		8		4				1
		5		1		3		
6				8		5		
3		2	1	6	7	8	4	9
4	6	9		3	8	1	5	7
1		7	4	9	5	2		6

Puzzle: 17

	7	8	4	3	6	5	1	2
5	2	4	8	7		6	9	3
3	1	6						
	6	5		4		2	3	8
	9	7		2		1	4	
2	4	3		1		7	5	
						8	2	4
4	3	1		8	2	9	6	5
6	8	2	5	9	4	3	7	

Puzzle: 18

5	8						6	2
9	1	2	6		4	7	3	5
6	7	4	3	5	2	9	1	8
7	3			4			9	6
			7	9	5			
8	2			3			4	7
1	4	8	5	2	3	6	7	9
2	9	6	8		7	3	5	4
3	5						8	1

Puzzle: 19

9	5		7		4		2	8
7	8	3	1		2	9	4	5
6	2	4	8		9	3	1	7
		6	5		3	8		
2				4				1
		5	9		1	4		
1	9	2	3		6	5	7	4
3	6	7	4		5	2	8	9
5	4		2		7		6	3

Puzzle: 20

4	5	1	9		7	6	2	3
	9	3	4	1	6	5	7	
8	7	6	2	5	3	9	4	1
			3		5			
		4		2		3		
			1		8			
5	1	2	8	9	4	7	3	6
	4	7	5	3	2	8	1	
9	3	8	6		1	4	5	2

Puzzle: 21

7	5			9			8	6
2	6	9	1		8	3	4	5
8	1	3	6		5	9	2	7
	3		4		6		7	
4			3	1	2			9
	2		9		7		3	
5	4	8	7		1	2	9	3
3	7	6	8		9	5	1	4
1	9			3			6	8

Puzzle: 22

8		2	7		9	1		4
3	5	7	6		1	8	2	9
1	9	4	8		5	3	6	7
			3		7			
2	3	1		6		4	7	5
			4		2			
7	4	3	2		6	5	9	1
6	1	9	5		4	2	8	3
5		8	1		3	7		6

8	6	3	7		2	4	5	9
4	9	2	6		5	1	3	7
5	7						2	6
	5	8		3		2	6	
1			9	2	8			3
	2	7		5		9	4	
6	8						9	4
2	3	4	8		9	7	1	5
7	1	9	5		3	6	8	2

1	4	9	7		6	3	8	2
6	5	2	4		3	1	7	9
	3	7		2		5	4	
		5	8		4	2		
2	1			9			3	8
		4	6		2	7		
	6	3		7		8	1	
4	2	8	3		1	9	5	7
5	7	1	9		8	6	2	3

	9	7	1	6	3	8	5	
5	1	3	9		4	2	6	7
4	6	8	7	5	2	9	3	1
		2				1		
	4			3			8	
		6				3		
6	2	1	4	7	8	5	9	3
9	8	4	3		5	6	7	2
	3	5	6	2	9	4	1	

2	3	6	9		1	7	5	8
	9	5		7		2	1	
7	1	8	5		3	4	6	9
		3	2	8	5	1		
			3	1	4			
		2	6	9	7	3		
5	2	9	7		8	6	4	1
	8	1		5		9	3	
3	7	4	1		9	8	2	5

Puzzle: 27

	8	1				7	3	
3	7	4	6		8	1	5	9
5	9	2				4	8	6
8	6	3	4		5	2	7	1
	1			6			4	
4	2	9	3		1	8	6	5
1	5	8				6	9	7
9	3	6	1		7	5	2	4
	4	7				3	1	

Puzzle: 28

3		1	5	2	6	4	9	8
	5	8		4	9		6	3
4		6	3	8	7	1	2	5
			7	5	1			
	1		8	6	3		7	
			2	9	4			
1	3	4	6	7	2	8		9
8	2		4	1			6	3
7	6	5	9	3	8	2		1

Puzzle: 29

5	7	3	9	1	4	2	6	8
2	1	8	7		3	9	5	4
	4	9		5		7	3	
	8	4				5	1	
			4	8	1			
	2	6				8	4	
	3	2		4		1	8	
4	5	1	8		6	3	9	7
8	6	7	1	3	9	4	2	5

Puzzle: 30

4	6	8				3	2	9
3	2						1	7
1	7	5	2	3	9	6	4	8
9	8	2	5		1	7	3	6
				2				
5	3	4	8		7	2	9	1
8	5	6	3	9	4	1	7	2
7	9						6	4
2	4	1				9	5	3

Puzzle: 31

5	2	4	1	7	8	3	9	
9		3	2	6		5		
6	8	1	5	9	3		2	7
		5	3	4		6		8
		7		2		1		
1		8		5	7	2		
3	4		7	8	5	9	1	2
		9		3	2	7		5
	5	2	9	1	6	8	3	4

Puzzle: 32

6			5	1	3	4	7	8
1	5	4	8	6	7	3		2
3			9		2	6	5	1
2	4	1	7					
8			1	2	4			9
					8	1	2	4
5	1	3	6		9			7
4		8	2	3	5	9	1	6
9	2	6	4	7	1			3

Puzzle: 33

4	3	1				7	5	9
9		2		1		4		6
5	6	7	4		3	2	1	8
6	7	3				9	2	4
1	5			2			8	7
2	9	8				5	6	1
3	2	9	1		6	8	7	5
7		6		8		1		2
8	1	5				6	4	3

Puzzle: 34

2	9	3	7		1	6	5	8
5	4	8		3		1	7	9
6		1		9		2		4
7	8	2				5	4	1
			5	7	2			
9	3	5				7	6	2
4		9		2		3		5
3	5	7		8		4	2	6
8	2	6	3		4	9	1	7

2	6	3	8	9		5	4	1
5	7	4	1	6			8	3
	1	8	4	3	5	2	7	6
				5			6	
8	9			1			2	5
	4			2				
6	8	1	2	4	3	7	5	
7	5			8	1	4	3	2
4	3	2		7	9	6	1	8

6	3	2	9		1	5	7	4
7	5		2		4		3	9
9	8	4				2	1	6
1	6		5		7		9	2
			4	9	8			
5	4		6		2		8	3
3	2	7				9	6	8
8	9		3		6		4	7
4	1	6	8		9	3	2	5

	4	3	7		2	9	8	
8	7	9	3		5	2	4	1
5	2	1	4		9	3	6	7
4			8	3	7			6
				2				
1			5	9	6			2
3	8	4	6		1	7	2	9
2	6	5	9		8	1	3	4
	1	7	2		3	6	5	

5	3	6	7		1	8	9	2
8	1	7	3		2	6	4	5
	4	2		6		1	7	
		8	2	1	6	9		
			4	5	3			
		1	8	7	9	5		
	6	3		8		4	2	
2	9	5	6		4	7	8	1
1	8	4	9		7	3	5	6

Puzzle: 39

4	9		5	2	6		7	3
			9		8			
			3	4	7			
9		2				4		7
		7	4		3	2		
8		3				9		5
			1	7	9			
			2		5			
7	2		6	3	4		8	9

Puzzle: 40

		6				8		
8		7				4		5
3		4	5	8	1	7		6
	4	8				9	7	
			7		9			
	6	9				3	5	
6		3	2	9	5	1		7
1		5				6		2
		2				5		

Puzzle: 41

			9	5	6			
9			2		3			8
		3	4	7	8	1		
2	6						9	7
		7	8		2	5		
5	9						1	3
		2	1	6	4	9		
8			7		5			1
			3	8	9			

Puzzle: 42

3			8	2	9			5
	8		3	4	5		7	
	9		7		6		3	
		6				2		
9			6		2			7
		3				5		
	5		9		3		2	
	7		1	8	4		5	
6			2	5	7			4

Puzzle: 43

			8	6				
9	6	5	4			2		
			3	9		7		
	9		2				3	1
6	7	4	3		8	2	5	9
1	2			9		4		
	5		6	7				
	4			5	2	9	6	
				8	3			

Puzzle: 44

	7	4				1	6	
8		6				2		5
	1	5		7		8	3	
		3	8		6	7		
	2						5	
		9	2		3	4		
	3	2		6		5	8	
9		8				6		1
	6	7				9	2	

Puzzle: 45

				3	8		5	
8	5			6	9		4	
			7	2				
3	2			9		1		
4	8	9	5		3	6	7	2
		6		8			3	5
				7	6			
	4			8	5		9	6
	6			9	4			

Puzzle: 46

		6	8	3	2	5		
	3			7		1		6
7			5		4			2
		7	6		3	1		
3								6
		5	9		8	7		
8			2		5			7
	7		3		9		5	
		1	4	7	6	8		

Puzzle: 47

			4	1				
	5		2	6		9	4	
	3			5	9			
		4		7			1	9
5	8	9	3		1	4	6	7
6	7			8		5		
			6	9			7	
	1	3		4	2		8	
				3	5			

Puzzle: 48

	2			7			1	
6		5		8		9		7
1				9				6
		8	9	2	7	6		
	9			8		5		4
		2	6	4	3	1		
9				5				1
2		1		3		5		9
	8			6			3	

Puzzle: 49

	2		8		5		7	
3			9		1			6
			4	7	6			
1		2	5		7	6		3
		8				2		
6		3	2		9	4		7
			1	5	8			
8			6		2			4
	6		7		3		1	

Puzzle: 50

		4		9			3	
	1	9		7	2	8		6
8				5	3	2		
			6	8	7			
	6		3		5		1	
			9	4	1			
	5	2	1					9
2		1	7	3		5	6	
	8			6			1	

Puzzle: 51

			5	9	1			
			2		6			
	5	9	7			4	2	6
4		5	6		8	1		9
	2						4	
3		1	4		9	7		2
	4	3	9		7	6	5	
			8		2			
			3	4	5			

Puzzle: 52

	9	7		4		3		
				8				4
1		5		3		8		2
			4	2	8			
7	8	4	3		6	5	2	9
			9	5	7			
4		1		6		9		3
5				9				
		2		7		1	5	

Puzzle: 53

	2	9		3		5	6	
		8		6		7		
1			8	9	7			4
			5	4	2			
		5	7		3	9		
			9	8	6			
6			1	5	4			9
		4		2		6		
	9	1		7		2	4	

Puzzle: 54

8			3	1			2	
			4	5	8			
	5			9				7
	4		5	7	1	6	8	9
			8	2	9			
7	8	9	6	3	4		5	
1				5			6	
		5	1	6				
	6			8	7			1

Puzzle: 55

7			1		8			2
	1			3			8	
6	3	8	4		5	1	9	7
			9		2			
		1				3		
			3		1			
9	8	5	6		7	2	1	3
	4			5			7	
3			2		9			4

Puzzle: 56

2		8				3		9
6	7	3	1		9	8	5	4
			8	3	5			
1								6
			2		1			
9								5
			9	6	2			
5	2	4	3		7	9	6	1
7		6				2		8

Puzzle: 57

			5		4			
	8		2	6	1		5	
3		2	7	9	8	1		4
1								8
		8	6		2	4		
5								9
6		5	4	8	9	2		1
	4		1	7	5		8	
			3		6			

Puzzle: 58

				5		1		
		4	1	3				
3		5	2	8		7	4	
				6		9	8	
4	9	8	3		2	5	6	7
	5	1		9				
	3	6		7	1	2		4
				2	8	3		
		9		4				

Puzzle: 59

3	7	6		5	9	4		
	4		3		1			
8	6				5	2		
	9	1		7	3			
7								5
	8	5		9	7			
9	1				8	5		
	3		5		2			
2	5	4		1	6	3		

Puzzle: 60

	1		6	9	8		5	
				5				
	8	5		7		4	6	
		1		6		5		
5	7	6	3		4	8	9	2
		4		8		7		
	5	8		4		9	2	
				2				
	9		8	3	1		4	

Puzzle: 61

		2	8	6				
			9		1			
	3	8		4		5		
2			9	6	4			1
5	8	6	7		2	9	3	4
1			8	3	5			7
		7		5		6	1	
		9		2				
			6	7	1			

Puzzle: 62

	9					7		
	8	4	1		7	2	9	
7	3			4		6	5	
	2	3				9	8	
			8		6			
	5	7				3	1	
3	4			7			5	2
	6	2	5		4	7	3	
	7						4	

Puzzle: 63

	1		2	5	9			
	5			4			3	2
			8	3				
1				6		3		9
3	9	2	4		7	6	5	8
5		8		9				7
				7	3			
4	7			8			6	
			1	2	4		7	

Puzzle: 64

2		5	9		8	6		3
4			1	7	6			8
7	6						9	4
9								6
			3		4			
8								5
6	9						3	1
5			8	3	9			7
3		4	7		1	5		9

Puzzle: 65

			2	8	3			
6	8	7	4		9	3	5	2
	2						4	
	7			9			6	
9	6						3	7
	1			5			2	
	3						1	
2	9	1	7		5	6	8	3
			1	3	2			

Puzzle: 66

9	5	2		3		8	6	7
	8						3	
	3	7				4	9	
	6		2		1		4	
5								8
	4		8		9		1	
	2	5				9	7	
	7						8	
4	9	1		8		2	5	6

Puzzle: 67

1			8	6		5		7
	8			4			9	
2				9	7			
		2		5				8
5	3	1	4		8	6	7	9
7				1		4		
			9	3				5
	7			8			1	
4		9		7	5			3

Puzzle: 68

	2		7	3	8		1	
5			9		1			8
			5		4			
	7	1	6		9	2	8	
		4				1		
	8	9	1		7	6	5	
			4		2			
8			3		5			1
	1		8	7	6		2	

Puzzle: 69

3	8	1	2	7	9		6	
				5	3			
	2	7	4	8	6			
			3		4	6		9
	7		9		8		5	
6		9	7		5			
			5	3	2	4	9	
			6	4				
	6		8	9	7	2	1	5

Puzzle: 70

		3				9	1	
7		1		8		5		
5	6	8	9	3		7	4	2
				9		8		
	8	7	5			4	6	9
		4		6				
8	1	9		4	5	3	6	7
		5		7		4		1
	7	6				2		

Puzzle: 71

	5		4	7	9		2	
	4		3	8	2		6	
		3	6		5	7		
3			9		6			7
	8	5				4	9	
6			7		8			5
		2	8		1	3		
	3		2	9	4		7	
	6		5	3	7		8	

Puzzle: 72

8			5		3	2		
9			4	8	2	7	5	
		2	7	9	6			
	2	3			7			
	7	8	6			9	5	2
			2			3	6	
			9	6	5	1		
	3	9	8	7	1			5
		6	3		4			9

Puzzle: 73

	6		9	3	4	2		5
		2						
3				7				
7	2		8	6	3	5	9	4
5	3	4				6	2	8
8	9	6	2	4	5		3	7
				1				9
					4			
4			9	7	2	8		5

Puzzle: 74

			2	5	3			
		8	6			4	5	
3			7	9	8			6
1	8		4		7		5	9
9		3				6		7
4	7		9		5		8	3
5			3	7	1			4
		4	5			6	9	
			8	4	9			

6	8		5	3	2	4	7	9
5		4		8				6
2							3	
9			1		7			5
7	1						4	3
8			9		3			1
	5							2
4				1		8		7
3	6	7	2	9	8		5	4

6	4		7		2		1	
		9	5				2	
	7		6	8	9		4	
			3	7	6			
7	9	3	2		4	5	8	6
			8	9	5			
	2		4	6	8		5	
	8			3	2			
	5		9		7		3	1

	3		7			4	8	
8	6	9	5	3		2	7	1
4	7						5	
				5			6	9
	5		4		7		3	
7	2			9				
	8						2	4
6	9	7		4	3	5	1	8
	4	5			1		9	

7	5	8	1	3	9		6	4
9				5				7
			7					9
6			3		2	1		8
4	8						2	5
2		7	9		5			3
1				4				
8				1				6
5	6		8	9	7	4	3	1

		6	8				5	
	2						6	
4	5	7		3	9	1	2	8
	7			5		3	9	6
	6		3		4		7	
1	8	3		9			4	
5	9	8	4	7		6	3	2
	4						8	
	3				5	7		

7	6	3	9	4	1		5	8
9		5						7
					5		6	9
2		4		3				5
5			7		8			3
6				5		8		1
3	7		5					
8						1		4
4	9		3	8	2	5	7	6

6	7		2	9	3	8	4	5
2					4			7
9				8				
4	5			1				6
7		8	5		9	1		3
3				7			5	9
				3				2
5			4					8
8	2	3	6	5	7		1	4

		9	7		5	6		
2			8	3	4			1
	1		2	9	6		7	
	5		6		8		9	
7		8				2		4
	6		9		2		3	
	4		3	6	9		2	
6			5	8	1			9
		3	4		7	5		

Puzzle: 83

				7	3	8		
	3		8	9	5		6	
	8		6	4	2		7	9
			2		7	9	8	
		8	4		6	2		
	5	7	9		8			
1	2		5	8	4		9	
	4		7	6	9		3	
		6	3	2				

Puzzle: 84

		4				9		
			2	5		7		
5	2	9	7	8	4	6		3
		6		9		3	4	
	7	8	4		1	2	5	
	4	2		3		8		
8		3	6	7	5	4	9	2
		5		4	3			
		7				5		

Puzzle: 85

3	8	1	2	7	9		6	
				5	3			
	2	7	4	8	6			
			3		4	6		9
	7		9		8		5	
6		9	7		5			
			5	3	2	4	9	
			6	4				
	6		8	9	7	2	1	5

Puzzle: 86

		3				9	1	
7		1		8		5		
5	6	8	9	3		7	4	2
				9		8		
	8	7	5		4	6	9	
		4		6				
8	1	9		4	5	3	6	7
		5		7		4		1
	7	6				2		

Puzzle: 87

	5		4	7	9		2	
	4		3	8	2		6	
		3	6		5	7		
3			9		6			7
	8	5				4	9	
6			7		8			5
		2	8		1	3		
	3		2	9	4		7	
	6		5	3	7		8	

Puzzle: 88

8			5		3	2		
9			4	8	2	7	5	
		2	7	9	6			
	2	3			7			
	7	8	6		9	5	2	
			2			3	6	
			9	6	5	1		
	3	9	8	7	1			5
		6	3		4			9

Puzzle: 89

	6		9	3	4	2		5
		2						
3				7				
7	2		8	6	3	5	9	4
5	3	4				6	2	8
8	9	6	2	4	5		3	7
				1				9
						4		
4			9	7	2	8		5

Puzzle: 90

			2	5	3			
		8	6			4	5	
3			7	9	8			6
1	8		4		7		5	9
9		3				6		7
4	7		9		5		8	3
5			3	7	1			4
		4	5			6	9	
			8	4	9			

Puzzle: 91

6	8		5	3	2	4	7	9
5		4		8				6
2							3	
9			1		7			5
7	1						4	3
8			9		3			1
	5							2
4				1		8		7
3	6	7	2	9	8		5	4

Puzzle: 92

6	4		7		2		1	
		9	5				2	
	7		6	8	9		4	
			3	7	6			
7	9	3	2		4	5	8	6
			8	9	5			
	2		4	6	8		5	
	8			3	2			
	5		9		7		3	1

Puzzle: 93

4	9	2	6	7	8	3		5
				4	5			9
8								7
5	3			2				6
6	2		1		4		7	8
7				9			3	4
3								2
2			9	5				
9		5	7	8	2	4	6	3

Puzzle: 94

			6	8	9			
		9	2	4	5	3		
6	5		7		3		8	4
9			5		8			2
4	3					5	7	
5			4		7			3
1	7		9		4		3	8
		3	8	5	6	1		
			3	7	1			

	1	5					8	
6	9		8	4	3	1	5	7
	4				5			3
	6	4		8			9	
	7		4		6		1	
	5			2		8	6	
4			9				3	
9	8	1	5	3	7		4	6
	3					9	7	

	2	1	9	5				
		6	1	8	4		9	
			6	2	7			5
			2	4	9		7	3
	1		7		8		5	
9	7		5	6	1			
6			8	9	5			
	9		4	1	6	2		
			7	2	5	6		

		9			3	5		
		7		4				
8		6	5	9	2	7	4	3
1		2		6		4		
	6	8	3		1	2	7	
		3		2		8		1
9	2	4	7	3	5	6		8
				8		9		
		5	6			3		

	3		8	4	1			
	9			3		2		
4				6		5		
7	4		3	2	5	8	9	6
	6		4		8		2	
2	8	5	6	7	9		4	3
		3		8				2
		7		9			5	
			1	5	3		6	

Puzzle: 99

		9		8			3	
7		5				2		
	8			7			9	1
			9	1	7			
9		6	4		8	5		7
			3	6	5			
4	1			5			6	
		7				8		4
	5			4		1		

Puzzle: 100

3			8	4		5		
	5	7		6				3
6			7	3		9		
	6			8				
	8	5				2	7	
			5				9	
		4		9	6			1
1				2		8	5	
		9		7	8			6

Puzzle: 101

9				5	8			7
		7	3	6				
				2			8	
3				7			5	
2	4	5	9		6	3	7	8
	8			4				6
	3			8				
				9	5	6		
1				7	3			5

Puzzle: 102

						4		
		7	3	5		1		
4	2			7			6	
			8	4	5		3	
	7	3	6		9	8	4	
	8		7	2	3			
	3			8			1	6
	8		9	6	2			
	2							

Puzzle: 103

3			8	7				2
	7			2	1	8		
		6		4	3			
								4
5	2	9	7		4	6	1	8
6								
			6	1		2		
		1	4	5			8	
4				8	9			1

Puzzle: 104

			4	2		8		
		6		8				
9				3			2	
			3	4	7			6
6	9	7	2		8	4	5	3
1			5	9	6			
	3			6				8
				7		2		
		8		5	3			

Puzzle: 105

						2		
	8		4	5		9	1	
2	4			3				
			9	1	6		2	
	7	1	8		3	4	9	
	2		5	4	7			
				9			4	7
	5	2		7	1		8	
		9						

Puzzle: 106

2				5				6
	9		7	6			2	
		6				3		
			4	3	7		5	
7	6			9			3	8
	5		6	8	2			
		1				8		
	2			4	9		7	
3				7				9

Puzzle: 107

5					7			2
	7		2	8			3	
				5				
9			4	2	6		8	
	6	8	3		5	9	7	
	4		8	7	9			3
				9				
	2			3	8		5	
3			5					1

Puzzle: 108

6		7			8			
					4	1	7	
		9		1	3			
			4	8	9		5	6
	4		3		5		1	
5	9		1	7	6			
			9	6		8		
	7	3	8					
			5			2		4

Puzzle: 109

2				1	8		5	3
6	1			9			2	
				4				
1				2				
8	9	2	6		4	7	1	5
				8				6
				7				
	6			5			8	1
9	5		4	6				2

Puzzle: 110

1		5	1	9		7	2	
				6		3		5
7				5				
	2	6	3	4			8	
	7						4	
	4		8	9	6	5		
			7					2
1		3	2					
	8	7	3	6	9			

Puzzle: 111

				8		1		
	2		6	3			8	
8			7	1				
				9		4	1	
3	5	4	1		7	8	6	9
	6	9		5				
				7	1			4
	8			6	9		2	
		6		4				

Puzzle: 112

1								9
	9	3		7			4	
			6	9			8	
			5	6	7	4		
	8	7	1		4	9	6	
		4	2	8	9			
	1			2	5			
	2			4		1	9	
8								2

Puzzle: 113

		2	7	6			4	
		5	1	3				
		3		8	2			
6			2	1	4		3	
4								1
	3		9	7	8			6
			6	4		2		
			2	3	9			
	1		9	7	3			

Puzzle: 114

	4	7				1		
			7					9
2		5		9		3		6
			1	4	6		2	
		6	8		7	9		
	8		5	2	9			
1		9		8		2		4
8					1			
		2				7	1	

		5					6	
6	9			4	7		5	
				5				8
	4		8	3	6			
	6	3	4		5	7	8	
			7	9	2		3	
9				7				
	8		9	2			7	1
	2				3			

	1			3		2		
		4		8				6
3					5		1	
		1	7	2	9			
5	2			4			6	7
			5	6	8	1		
	9			8				4
6				9		7		
		5		4			3	

1		9				5	4	2
6								
2			1		4			7
		2	4	8	5	7		
			2		6			
		1	3	9	7	6		
4			9		8			6
								9
9	2	7				8		4

		3	4	5		7	6	
4				2				
8				1				3
				8				4
7	1	6	9		3	2	8	5
5				6				
2				7				8
				3				2
	7	8		9	4	5		

1 = yellow   2 = orange   3 = light blue   4 = pink   5 = light green

6 = dark blue   7 = red   8 = dark green   9 = brown

DOT TO DOT

Grow more sunflowers.

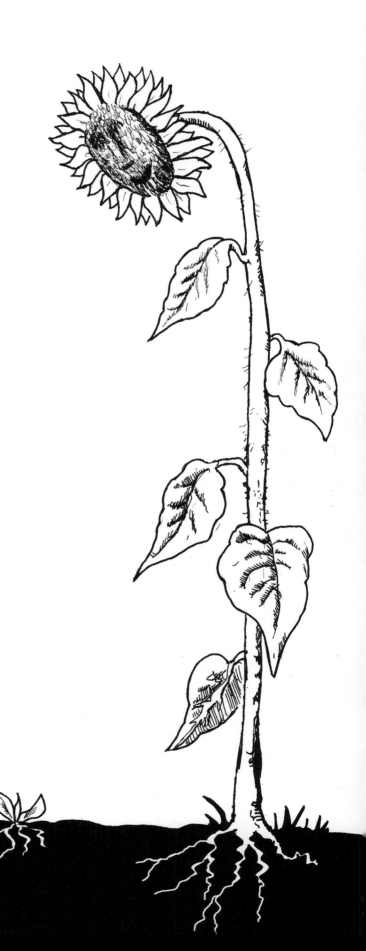

1 = dark green   2 = light green   3 = yellow   4 = orange

5 = red   6 = blue   7 = brown   8 = grey

DOT TO DOT

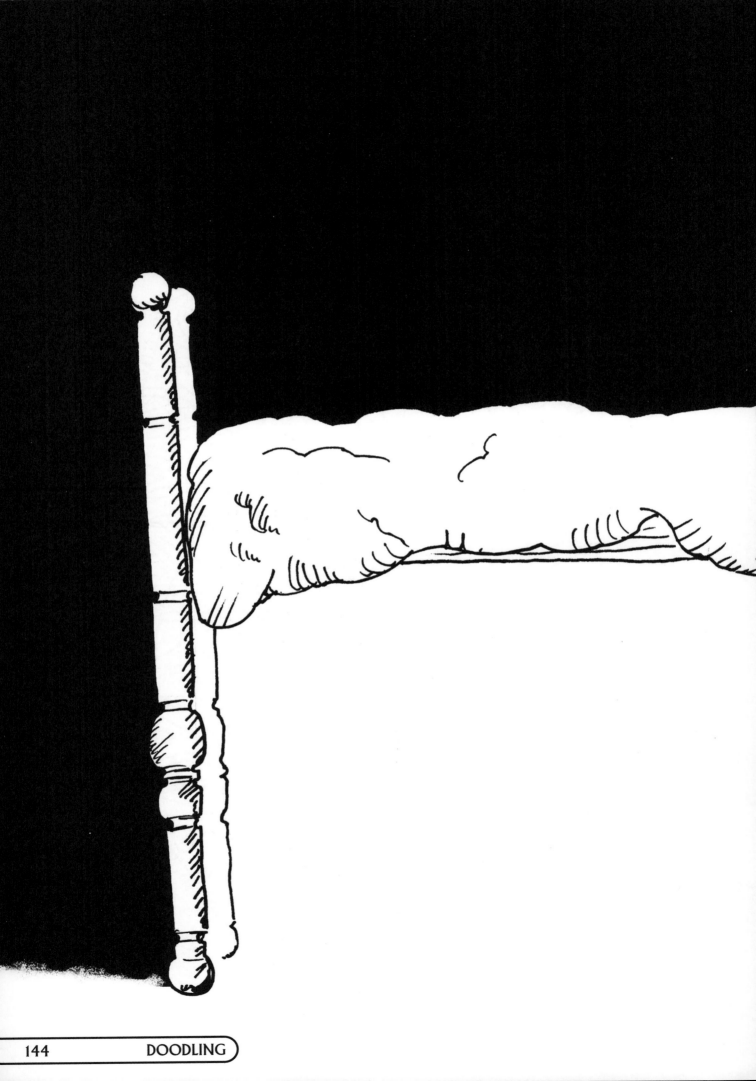

DOODLING

1 = yellow
2 = light green
3 = dark green
4 = blue
5 = orange
6 = red
7 = purple
8 = pink
9 = brown

Put a tail on the bird of paradise.

Paint the beach hut.

1 = dark brown   2 = light brown   3 = orange   4 = grey

5 = light green   6 = dark green   7 = pink   8 = yellow   9 = blue

Why is the cave man fleeing?

DOODLING

DOMINO CHAINS

To solve these puzzles, you need to use the dominos below the domino chain to fill in the gaps above.

There are two important things to remember:

1. Dominoes can only touch one another when the number of spots on their touching ends match.
2. You can only use the dominos shown underneath each domino chain, and you can only use each domino once.

When you have found the correct domino for an empty space, either draw an arrow showing where the domino should go, or draw the dots on yourself, and cross out the corresponding domino below.

If you get stuck and can't work out which domino goes where, don't panic – all of the answers are in the back of the book!

Puzzle: 1

Puzzle: 2

Puzzle: 3

Puzzle: 4

Puzzle: 5

Puzzle: 6

Puzzle: 7

Puzzle: 8

Puzzle: 9

Puzzle: 10

NUMBER SEARCHES

You'll need all your skill and cunning to solve these nauseating number searches.

All of the long numbers below are hidden in their corresponding grid. They could be arranged horizontally, vertically or diagonally. Can you find them?

If you get completely stuck and can't find a number, don't panic – all of the answers are in the back of the book.

Puzzle: 1

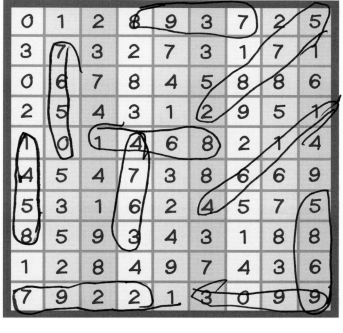

0	1	2	8	9	3	7	2	5
3	7	3	2	7	3	1	7	1
0	6	7	8	4	5	8	8	6
2	5	4	3	1	2	9	5	1
0	1	4	6	8	2	1	4	
4	5	4	7	3	8	6	6	9
5	3	1	6	2	4	5	7	5
8	5	9	3	4	3	1	8	8
1	2	8	4	9	7	4	3	6
7	9	2	2	1	3	0	9	9

Puzzle: 2

3	3	5	6	4	5	9	3	4
2	1	6	4	8	7	8	2	8
1	2	9	3	4	9	6	1	5
3	3	4	6	2	6	5	7	2
5	8	5	8	7	9	2	4	2
3	7	2	9	4	5	6	3	1
1	9	4	9	6	7	8	1	2
6	3	9	1	7	3	5	6	3
9	6	6	5	0	7	6	4	8
5	1	9	8	4	1	2	4	6

Puzzle 1 numbers:

1468	3099	9685
8937	8541	1164
7650	2297	
2875	4763	

Puzzle 2 numbers:

2568	3356	5961
5699	2584	2387
1246	7546	
6592	9986	

Puzzle: 3

3	4	8	6	4	5	9	5	2
1	6	4	6	8	3	2	1	2
9	9	4	9	7	2	6	6	3
3	7	2	3	9	7	1	8	6
6	9	8	2	4	8	5	2	3
6	1	7	8	7	1	4	6	9
8	2	2	4	6	7	3	5	7
5	5	3	4	5	3	2	4	8
7	4	9	1	2	4	8	6	3
9	8	3	5	2	8	9	4	1

2894	6685	1254
5464	5468	6187
2236	6683	
5489	4751	

Puzzle: 4

1	1	2	5	3	1	3	6	3
9	3	2	4	5	7	1	3	4
1	3	5	6	4	2	5	8	5
9	4	6	5	9	7	3	2	6
8	3	9	2	6	4	8	3	1
7	2	9	4	8	3	9	5	7
6	8	9	5	3	2	2	1	8
7	5	6	4	4	1	3	5	8
2	7	8	3	8	7	6	4	5
6	1	2	4	6	9	1	4	4

5642	3357	6789
9965	5467	5644
4588	6392	
1246	1125	

Puzzle: 5

6	6	4	5	3	1	4	9	5
5	3	7	3	2	4	6	5	8
2	9	4	3	8	9	7	6	4
1	6	8	6	3	2	2	3	6
2	5	1	4	6	7	8	4	9
4	2	4	8	9	4	5	7	8
9	5	9	4	4	1	1	8	3
8	7	6	2	3	4	6	5	8
1	8	9	8	4	3	9	3	9
9	2	5	7	6	2	5	8	7

5846	5693	2465
2236	6645	8942
9864	9514	
2587	3648	

Puzzle: 6

9	2	1	9	3	1	6	8	1
1	4	8	9	6	3	6	2	1
6	2	5	3	2	7	4	5	3
3	1	8	4	9	8	5	9	5
2	8	6	2	3	5	9	2	1
9	3	7	5	6	4	7	9	5
4	2	4	7	5	6	2	8	8
7	6	5	4	1	5	2	6	3
6	1	9	8	5	8	6	2	2
4	8	7	7	6	5	9	7	4

2359	1135	9934
7854	5832	8771
8622	6749	
4697	3526	

Puzzle: 7

3	2	6	3	6	1	9	8	1
9	4	7	1	4	6	6	7	2
8	7	5	2	3	2	4	5	3
4	2	8	3	5	6	2	8	8
3	2	2	6	4	2	5	5	7
7	3	4	1	8	6	6	9	6
1	8	6	9	7	5	3	4	2
5	1	2	6	5	3	2	9	7
4	3	1	5	9	3	2	1	9
2	4	4	6	9	8	6	5	7

6672	9123	4318
3984	5621	1365
2516	7972	
4875	8669	

Puzzle 8

5	4	3	4	4	8	6	2	6
4	1	6	9	2	4	1	8	2
8	2	1	9	7	6	7	1	3
1	3	1	6	3	2	9	5	6
8	5	9	4	1	8	3	3	7
5	5	7	6	2	4	6	5	2
9	2	4	7	5	8	7	3	1
3	6	9	7	3	1	1	8	4
8	2	1	3	6	8	7	9	6
9	1	5	7	2	5	3	9	7

3128	6236	1976
4652	7911	1845
8197	8443	
5576	2972	

Puzzle: 9

3	5	1	3	4	5	1	8	4
7	2	8	6	2	7	8	6	2
1	5	7	4	3	6	7	1	6
6	8	3	2	1	9	5	4	3
7	7	2	5	4	3	8	7	9
8	2	4	6	1	6	5	2	2
2	4	1	6	6	8	7	3	8
4	9	4	1	4	5	5	9	1
6	8	3	5	7	3	9	4	6
4	2	8	1	2	6	7	1	4

4367	1423	1824
9281	8758	3272
6659	7346	
2876	4815	

Puzzle: 10

3	5	7	6	7	9	1	4	3
1	7	8	4	4	7	9	4	2
3	1	2	9	4	5	3	4	2
2	5	3	1	2	9	8	8	8
1	6	5	9	8	4	3	3	4
1	6	8	6	4	1	9	2	2
4	4	5	1	3	2	4	6	5
8	9	6	4	6	3	7	8	9
3	5	1	7	9	4	5	7	1
8	8	6	2	2	3	3	8	3

3576	4483	8862
6491	5946	2482
7629	6942	
3383	3211	

1 = blue   2 = orange   3 = red   4 = pink   5 = purple   6 = yellow

1 = yellow   2 = orange   3 = blue   4 = pink
5 = red   6 = purple   7 = light green   8 = dark green

DOT TO DOT

Design a great gadget.

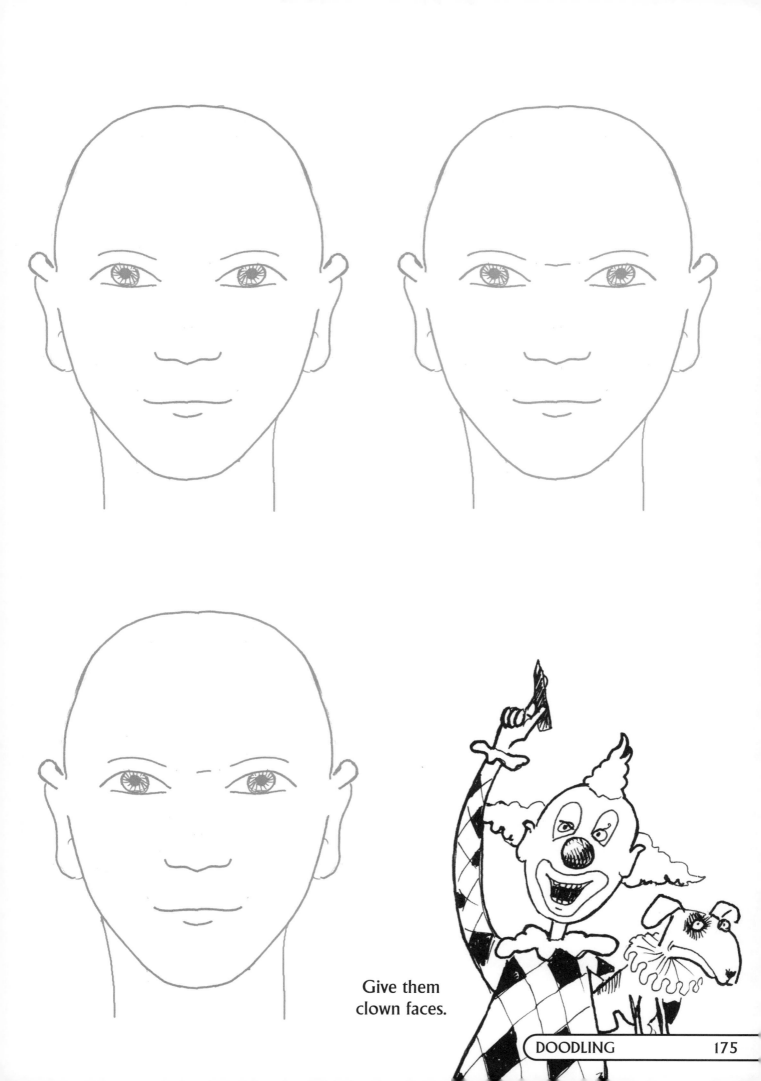

Give them
clown faces.

1 = yellow   2 = red   3 = blue   4 = purple   5 = pink   6 = orange

1 = dark green   2 = dark blue   3 = light green
4 = pink   5 = light blue   6 = purple   7 = yellow

DOT TO DOT

What went bang in the night?

1 = pink   2 = green   3 = orange   4 = yellow

5 = red   6 = blue   7 = brown

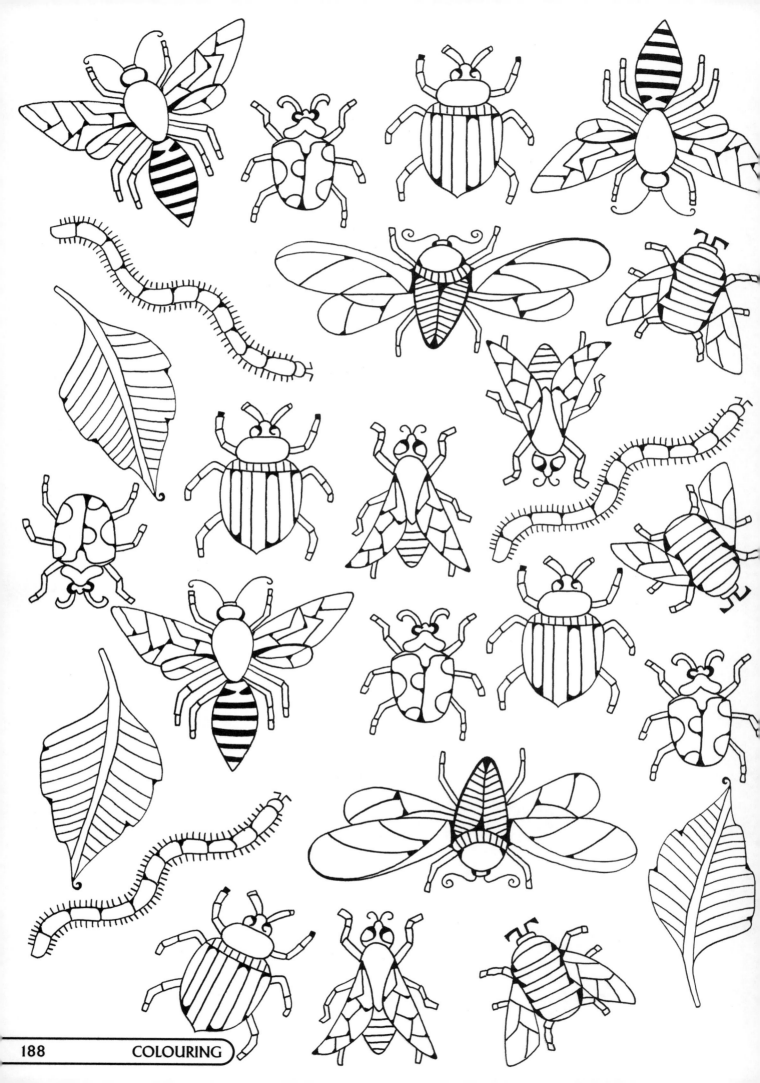

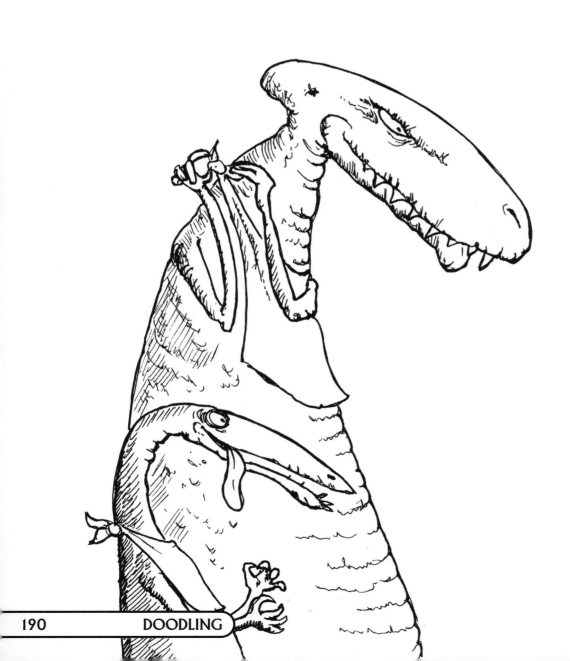

DOODLING

Draw their dinner.

TAI-CHI TOWERS

Have you got what it takes to tackle a Tai-Chi Tower?

Every number in a box is a sum of the two numbers in the boxes beneath it added together. Fill in each empty box with the correct number to complete the tower.

There are two ways of figuring out the missing numbers. You can either add the two numbers below the empty box together or minus the number beside the empty box from the number they share above.

If you get completely stuck and can't work one out, don't panic – all of the answers are in the back of the book!

Puzzle: 1   Puzzle: 2

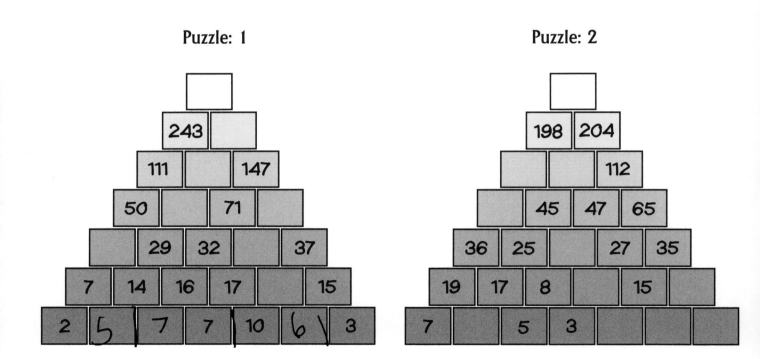

Puzzle: 3

- Row (top): [ ]
- 155, 133, [ ]
- 91, 64, [ ], 77
- [ ], 33, 31, [ ], 39
- [ ], [ ], 11, 20, 18, 21
- [ ], [ ], 3, [ ], [ ], 6, 15

Puzzle: 4

- Row (top): [ ]
- 256, [ ]
- 128, 128, 152
- [ ], [ ], 66, [ ]
- 35, [ ], 31, [ ], 51
- [ ], [ ], [ ], 15, 20, 31
- 12, 8, [ ], [ ], [ ], [ ], 17

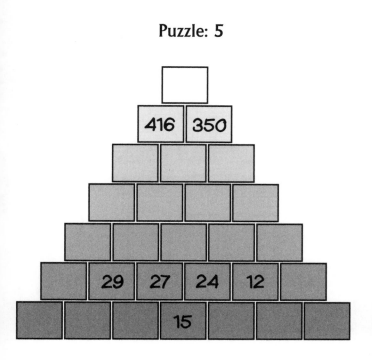

Puzzle: 5

- Row (top): [ ]
- 416, 350
- [ ], [ ], [ ]
- [ ], [ ], [ ], [ ]
- [ ], [ ], [ ], [ ], [ ]
- 29, 27, 24, 12, [ ]
- [ ], [ ], [ ], 15, [ ], [ ], [ ]

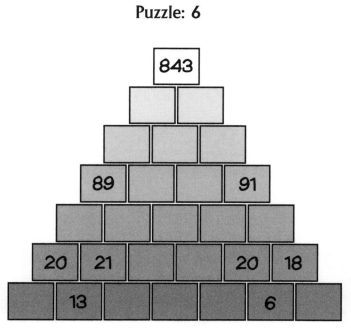

Puzzle: 6

- Row (top): 843
- [ ], [ ]
- [ ], [ ], [ ]
- 89, [ ], 91
- [ ], [ ], [ ], [ ]
- 20, 21, [ ], [ ], 20, 18
- [ ], 13, [ ], [ ], 6, [ ]

1 = orange
2 = yellow
3 = red
4 = grey
5 = purple
6 = blue
7 = green
8 = brown

What's in the haunted mine?

1 = black
2 = pink

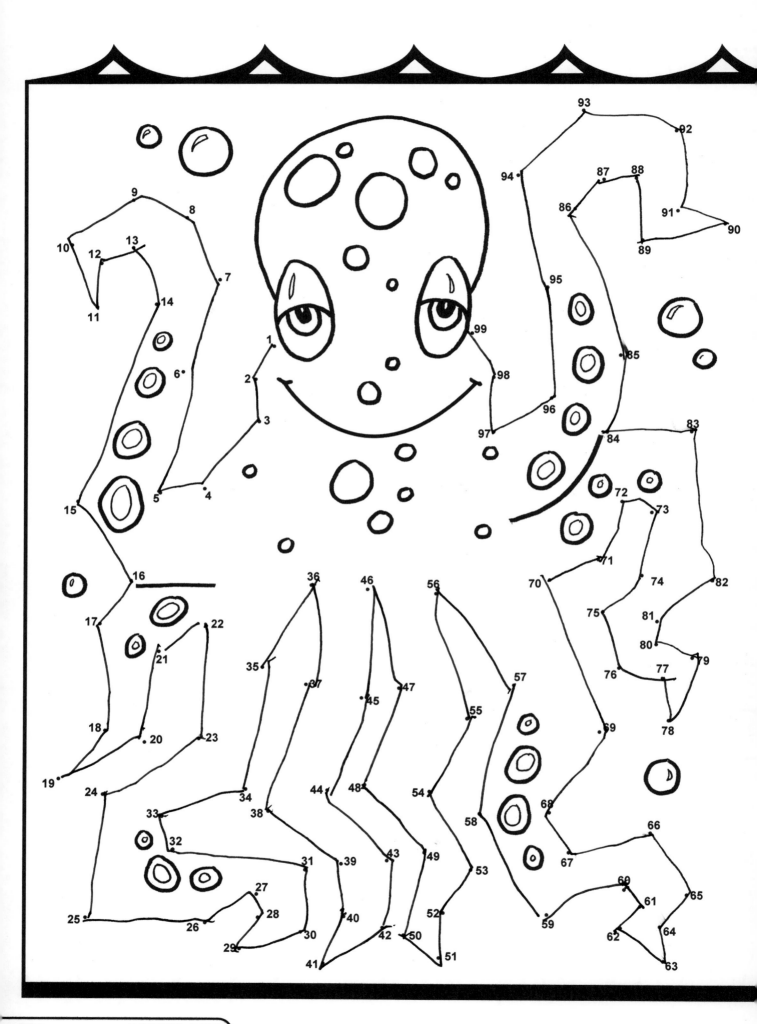

Design your dream ice cream.

DOODLING

What's his excuse?

1 = red   2 = yellow   3 = orange

4 = green   5 = blue   6 = purple

Launch the rocket.

10, 9, 8, 7, 6, 5, 4, 3, 2, 1,
LIFT OFF!

Where are they going to land?

1 = orange   2 = grey   3 = yellow   4 = green

5 = red   6 = blue   7 = brown   8 = purple

DOT TO DOT

Fill the mermaid's chest with treasure.

Sketch in some slimy specimens.

COSMIC CONNECTORS

Cosmic Connectors look like ordinary crosswords, but they have a twist! Instead of having clues written next to them, all the clues you need are contained within the puzzle.

All you have to do is fill in each empty box with a number from 1 to 9 to make all the sums correct. The sums need to work both across and down.

It is easiest to start with a row or column that only has one number missing.

If you get completely stuck and can't work one out, don't panic – all of the answers are in the back of the book.

Puzzle: 1

1	+	1	×	2	=	4
+	■	×	■	+	■	+
9	÷		+	2	=	5
−	■	−	■	−	■	−
4	+	2	÷	3	=	2
=	■	=	■	=	■	=
6	×	1	+	1	=	7

Puzzle: 2

7	×	2	−		=	9
+	■	×	■	+	■	−
4	÷	2	+		=	
−	■	×	■	−	■	+
	+		−	5	=	2
=	■	=	■	=	■	=
	+	4	−		=	6

Puzzle: 3

Puzzle: 4

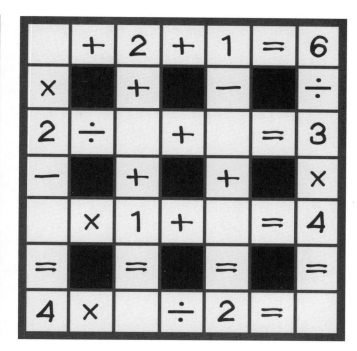

Puzzle: 5

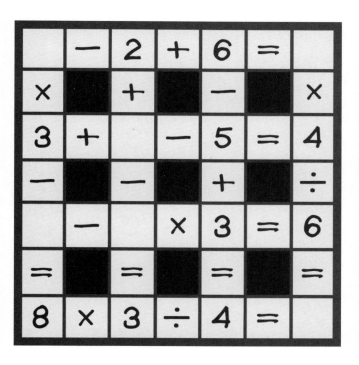

Puzzle: 6

Puzzle: 7

6	+		−	7	=	
−	■	+	■	−	■	+
4	−		+	4	=	3
+	■	−	■	+	■	+
	−	2	+	1	=	
=	■	=	■	=	■	=
5	+		−		=	7

Puzzle: 8

9	+		÷	2	=	
+	■	−	■	÷	■	÷
	×	6	−		=	4
−	■	+	■	+	■	×
7	−		×	1	=	3
=	■	=	■	=	■	=
	+	5	−		=	6

Puzzle: 9

5	×		−	8	=	2
+	■	×	■	×	■	×
	−	3	÷		=	2
÷	■	−	■	÷	■	+
7	+	5	÷		=	
=	■	=	■	=	■	=
	−	1	+		=	7

Puzzle: 10

	×	3	−	3	=	
×	■	×	■	+	■	×
3	+		−	3	=	
÷	■	−	■	+	■	÷
	+	2	+	2	=	6
=	■	=	■	=	■	=
6	×		÷	8	=	

PAPER CRAFT PROJECT

In this section there are lots of cool, crafty creations to cut out and complete.

On each right-hand page you will find the outlines of a new paper project for you to create.

First, turn the page and doodle a cool design on each of the shapes. Sometimes there will be doodling to be done on both sides of the page. You can use colouring pencils or felt-tip pens to complete and colour your creations.

Once you've finished doodling, turn the page back again. Now cut out each paper shape roughly, being careful to keep well away from the solid outside edges – this will make it easier to cut the pieces out neatly later on.

Make sure you keep all the instructions safe after you have finished cutting out. You will need these to help you make your paper project.

Finally, follow the step-by-step instructions to cut out your crafty creations and bring it to life!

CAREFUL CUTTING

 Always cut out the shapes on the right-hand page – the side of the page on which you see this scissors picture. This will ensure your final models don't have black lines showing around the edges.

Only cut along the solid lines that look like this: _____

SCORING SENSE

'Scoring' along a fold line creates a sharper crease, which helps each paper project to keep its shape or stand up by itself.

To score along a fold line, place a ruler along it and run an old ballpoint pen that has run out of ink along the edge, as shown here.

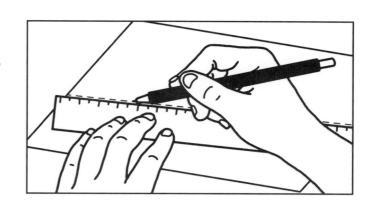

FOLDING RULES

There are two different types of fold line in this section.

Lines that look like this: – – – – – – – –
must be folded in a V-shape along the line, so
that the fold line is inside the fold.

Lines that look like this: · – · – · – · – ·
are reverse fold lines and should be folded in the
opposite direction, so that the fold line is on the
outside of the fold.

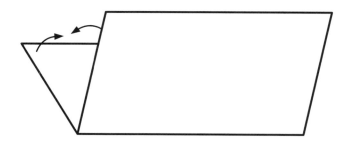

GLUE AREAS

These dark-grey shaded areas
show you where to put glue.

Glue area

Always apply a small dab of glue using a glue
stick, then press the glued area firmly on to
the paper, where marked.

The light-grey shaded areas
show you where to stick down
the glued area.

Glue
positioning
area

Leave each paper project to dry completely
before playing with it.

Big-Cat Straw-Toppers

Turn the page over and doodle your designs, then cut out your toppers below.
You will also need two drinking straws.

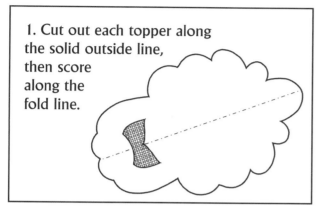

1. Cut out each topper along the solid outside line, then score along the fold line.

2. Fold each topper in half so that the design is on the inside, then cut out the shaded areas.

Shaded area

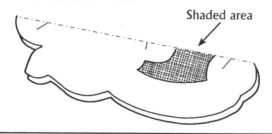

3. While your topper is still folded, make three little cuts, where shown.

4. Unfold each topper so that the design is on the outside, then thread it on to a straw.

Big-Cat Straw-Toppers

Why not give one big-cat straw-topper to a friend and keep the other for yourself? Next time you see each other you can slurp in style together!

Doodle more spots on the leopard.

Pop your finished straw-toppers in your favourite drinks and enjoy.

Give the lion a curly mane.

Spotty Frog

Finish the doodle design on this page and the next, then cut out your frog below.

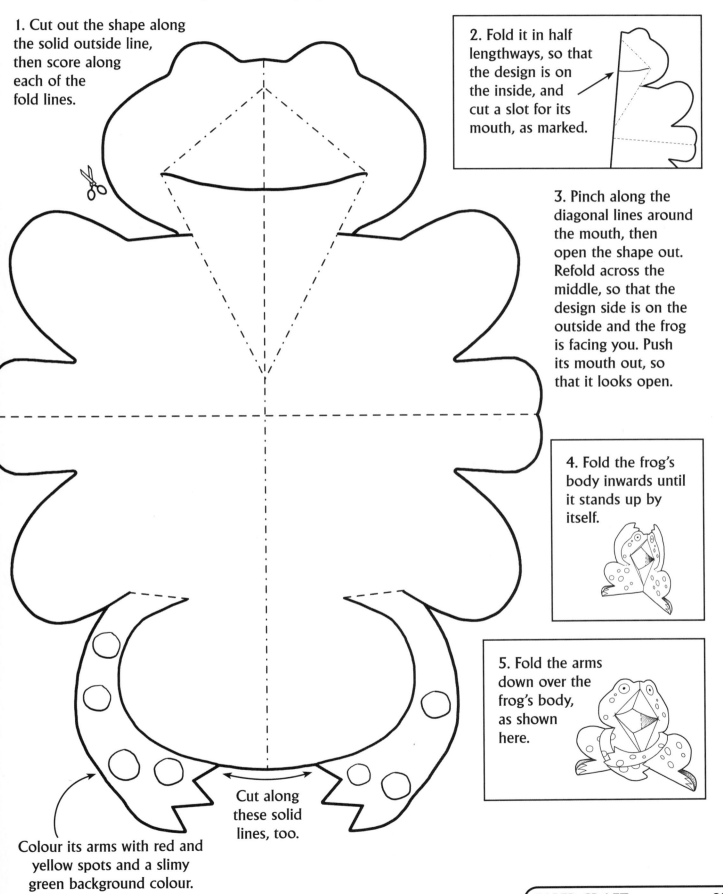

1. Cut out the shape along the solid outside line, then score along each of the fold lines.

2. Fold it in half lengthways, so that the design is on the inside, and cut a slot for its mouth, as marked.

3. Pinch along the diagonal lines around the mouth, then open the shape out. Refold across the middle, so that the design side is on the outside and the frog is facing you. Push its mouth out, so that it looks open.

4. Fold the frog's body inwards until it stands up by itself.

5. Fold the arms down over the frog's body, as shown here.

Cut along these solid lines, too.

Colour its arms with red and yellow spots and a slimy green background colour.

Spotty Frog

Some frogs have brightly coloured spots on their skin so that their enemies think that they won't taste nice or might be poisonous.

Add more spots to the frog's body and colour them in bright shades of red and yellow.

Fill in the skin around the spots so that it is a slimy green colour.

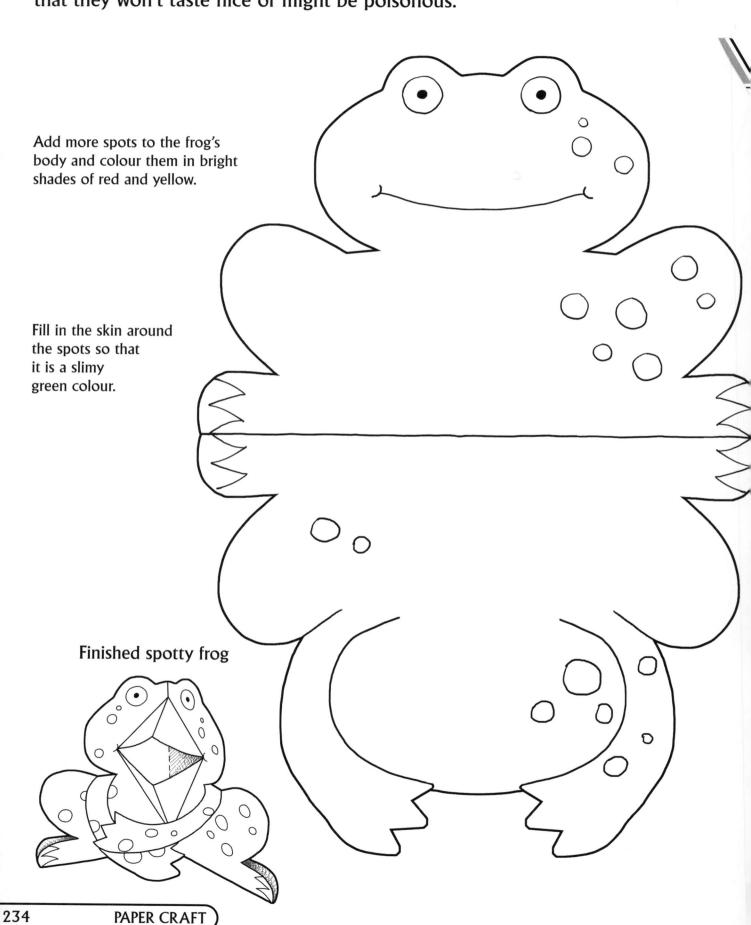

Finished spotty frog

Terrific Tortoise

Turn the page and doodle your design, then cut out your tortoise below.

1. Cut out the shape along the solid outside line, then score along each of the fold lines.

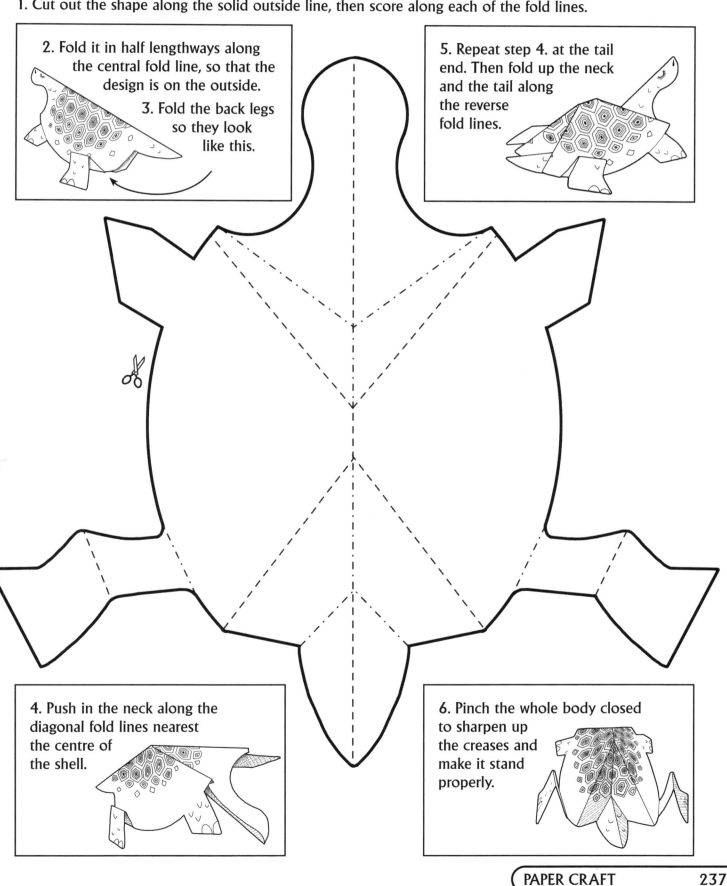

2. Fold it in half lengthways along the central fold line, so that the design is on the outside.

3. Fold the back legs so they look like this.

5. Repeat step 4. at the tail end. Then fold up the neck and the tail along the reverse fold lines.

4. Push in the neck along the diagonal fold lines nearest the centre of the shell.

6. Pinch the whole body closed to sharpen up the creases and make it stand properly.

Terrific Tortoise

A tortoise's shell is made of hard, bony plates that protect it from being eaten by hungry predators.

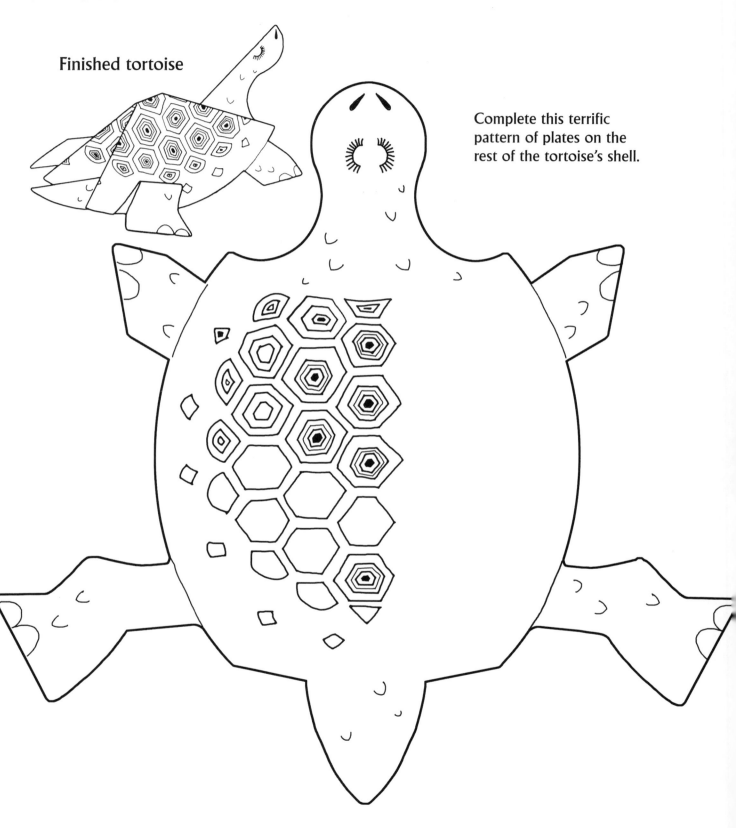

Finished tortoise

Complete this terrific pattern of plates on the rest of the tortoise's shell.

Giant Giraffe

Turn the page and doodle your design, then cut out your giraffe below.

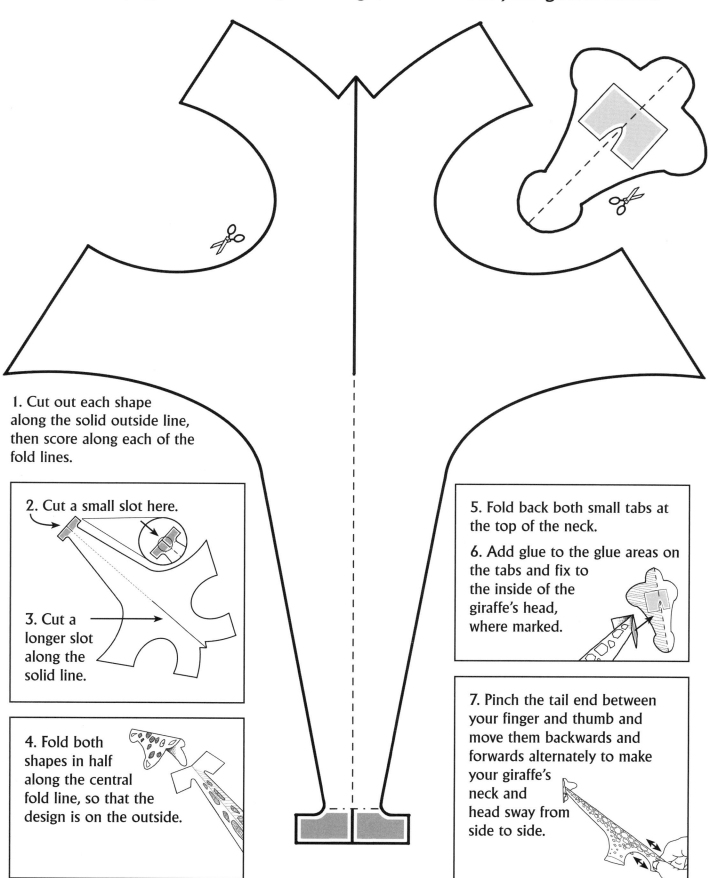

1. Cut out each shape along the solid outside line, then score along each of the fold lines.

2. Cut a small slot here.

3. Cut a longer slot along the solid line.

4. Fold both shapes in half along the central fold line, so that the design is on the outside.

5. Fold back both small tabs at the top of the neck.

6. Add glue to the glue areas on the tabs and fix to the inside of the giraffe's head, where marked.

7. Pinch the tail end between your finger and thumb and move them backwards and forwards alternately to make your giraffe's neck and head sway from side to side.

Giant Giraffe

Some scientists believe that giraffes have long necks to help them reach for food in tall trees. Others believe that they use their long necks as weapons to fight off rival giraffes.

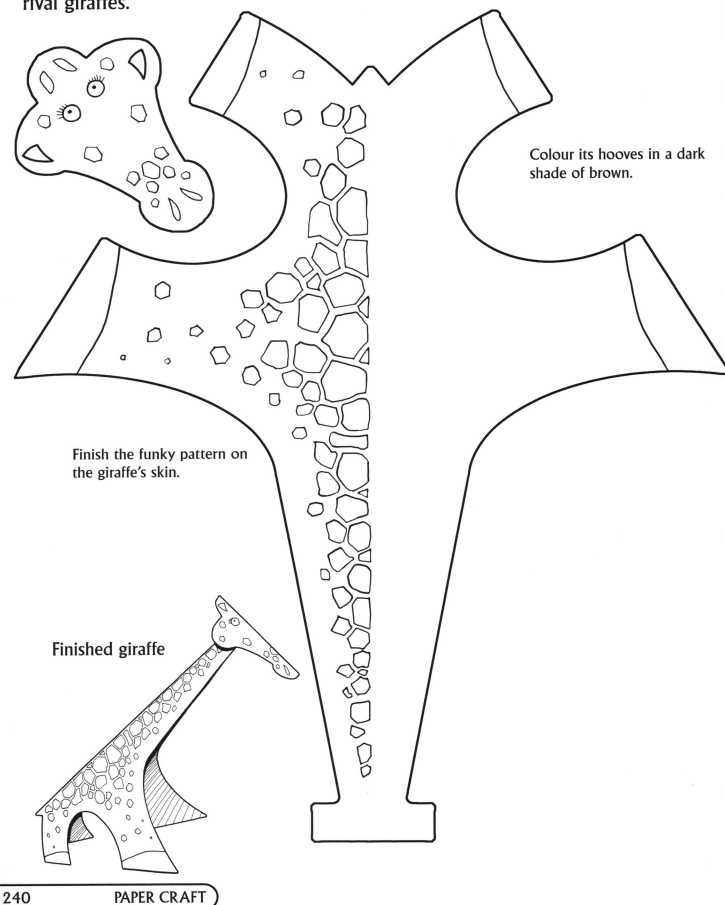

Colour its hooves in a dark shade of brown.

Finish the funky pattern on the giraffe's skin.

Finished giraffe

Awesome Owl

Turn the page and doodle your design, then cut out your owl below.

1. Cut out the shape along the solid outside line, then score along the fold lines.

2. Cut two small slots where the line is solid, as shown below.

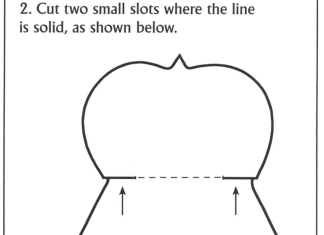

3. Fold all three fold lines in the same direction. The design should now be on the outside, as shown here.

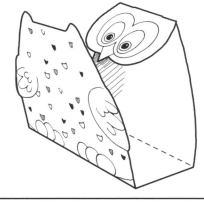

These are its feather tufts.

4. Flip the head over the front of the owl and fit the feather tufts through the slots on each side.

Awesome Owl

Owls hunt for their prey at night. They have special feathers so that they can fly silently without warning their prey.

Make its big eyes bright yellow.

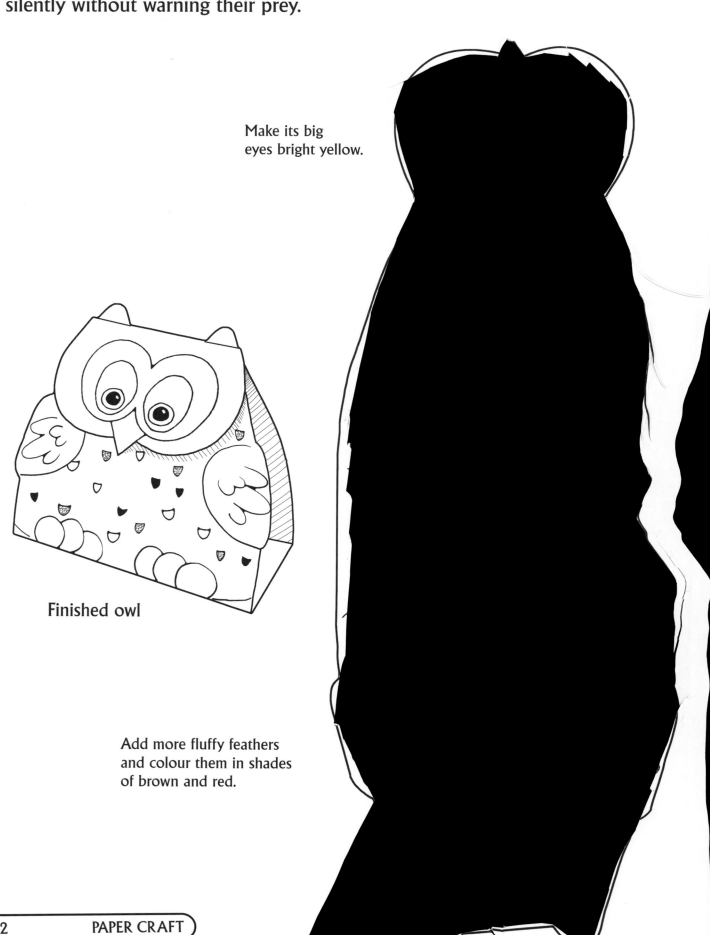

Finished owl

Add more fluffy feathers and colour them in shades of brown and red.

All The Answers

Crosswords pages 26-50

31 32 33 34 35
36 37 38 39 40
41 42 43 44 45
46 47 48 49 50
51 52 53 54 55
56 57 58 59 60

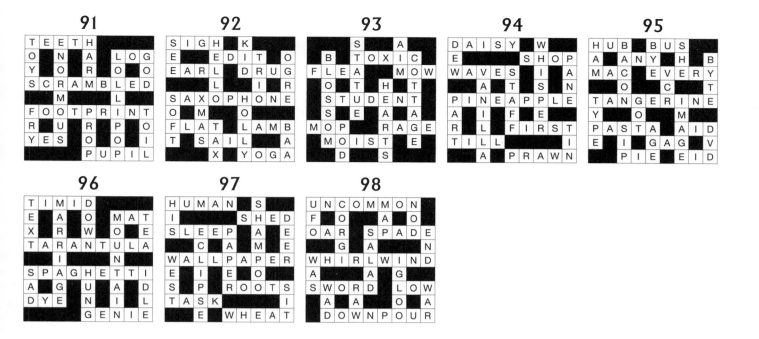

Wordsearches pages 63-87

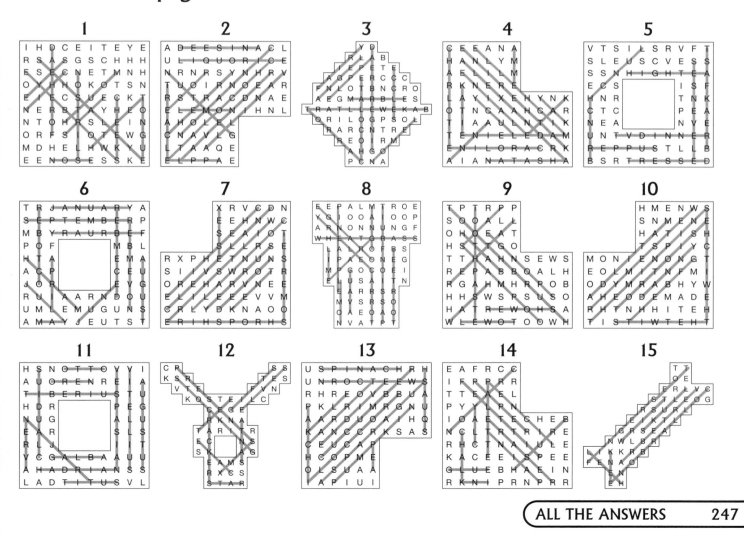

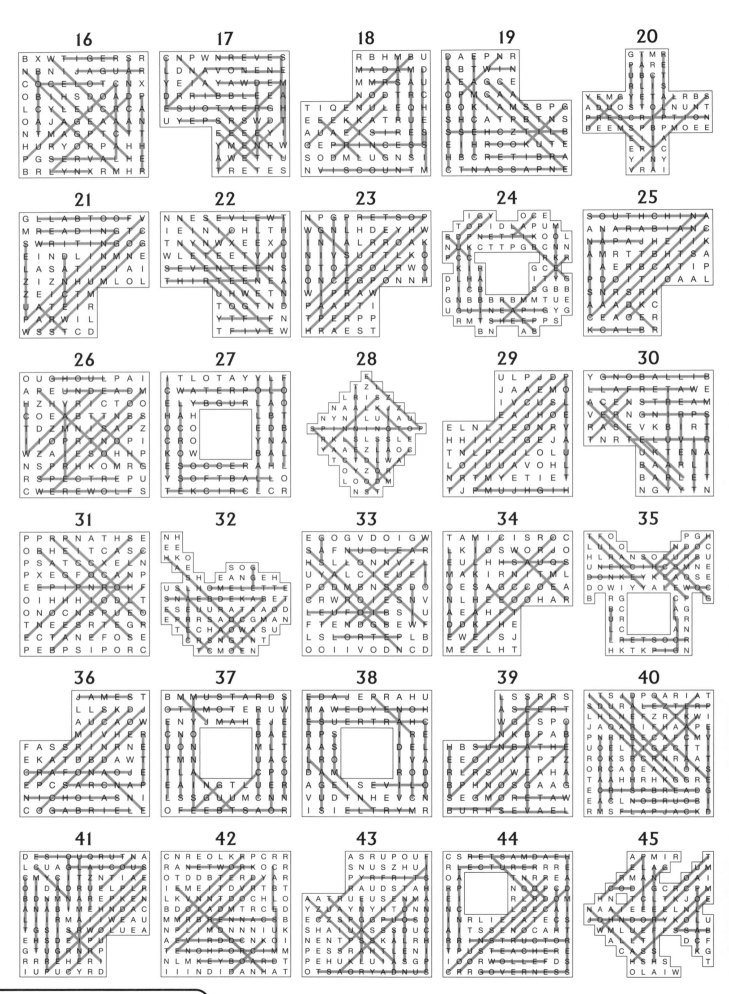

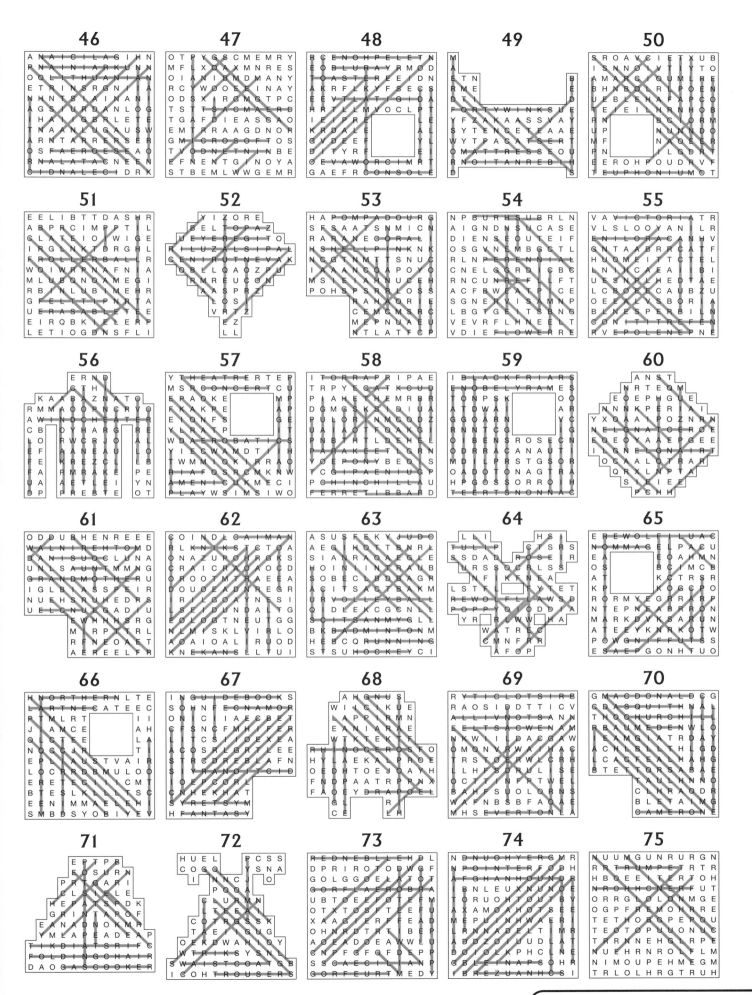

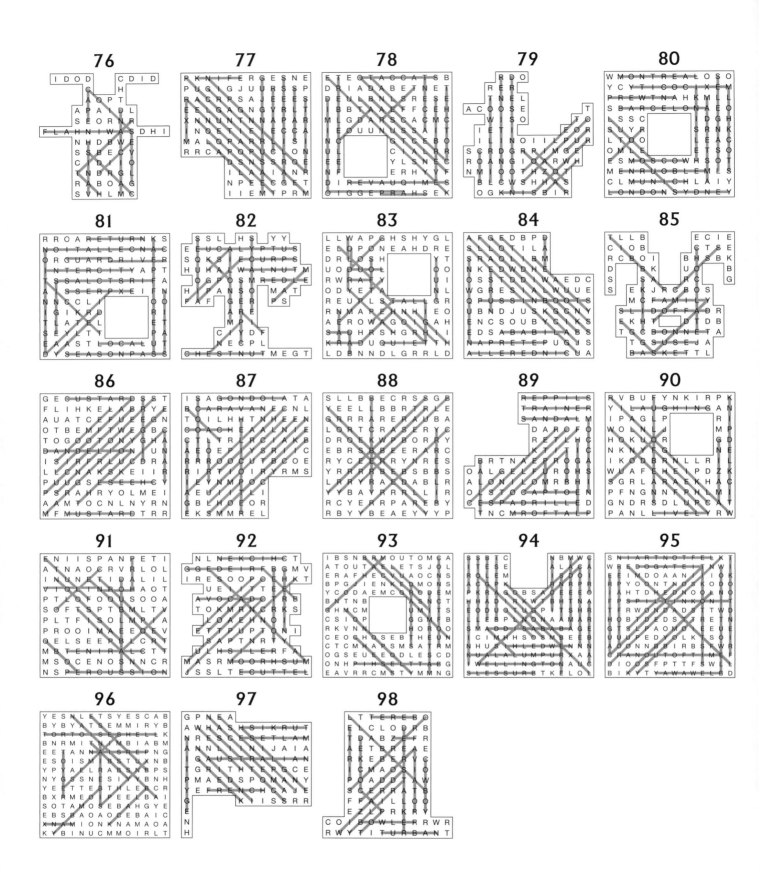

1
```
9 5 1 2 7 6 8 4 3
3 8 4 9 5 1 2 7 6
6 7 2 8 4 3 5 1 9
1 3 9 7 6 8 4 2 5
2 4 8 3 1 5 9 6 7
5 6 7 4 9 2 1 3 8
4 9 3 1 8 7 6 5 2
8 2 6 5 3 4 7 9 1
7 1 5 6 2 9 3 8 4
```

2
```
4 8 2 6 9 7 5 3 1
3 7 1 8 4 5 6 2 9
9 5 6 1 3 2 4 8 7
2 6 7 3 5 9 1 4 8
8 1 4 2 7 6 3 9 5
5 9 3 4 1 8 7 6 2
6 4 5 9 2 1 8 7 3
7 3 9 5 8 4 2 1 6
1 2 8 7 6 3 9 5 4
```

3
```
8 1 2 4 7 3 5 6 9
7 6 3 1 5 9 4 8 2
5 4 9 6 8 2 7 3 1
2 3 7 9 1 4 6 5 8
6 9 4 5 2 8 3 1 7
1 5 8 7 3 6 2 9 4
4 2 5 8 6 1 9 7 3
9 8 6 3 4 7 1 2 5
3 7 1 2 9 5 8 4 6
```

4
```
6 9 7 5 3 1 4 8 2
2 8 5 6 9 4 1 3 7
1 3 4 7 8 2 9 6 5
9 5 8 2 6 3 7 4 1
7 1 2 9 4 8 6 5 3
4 6 3 1 5 7 8 2 9
8 2 9 3 7 6 5 1 4
5 4 1 8 2 9 3 7 6
3 7 6 4 1 5 2 9 8
```

5
```
5 7 8 3 1 9 4 2 6
6 3 4 5 7 2 1 9 8
1 2 9 4 8 6 7 5 3
3 6 5 9 4 1 8 7 2
4 8 2 6 5 7 9 3 1
9 1 7 2 3 8 5 6 4
8 5 1 7 6 3 2 4 9
7 9 6 1 2 4 3 8 5
2 4 3 8 9 5 6 1 7
```

6
```
8 9 1 4 3 7 5 2 6
7 2 4 9 5 6 8 1 3
6 3 5 2 8 1 4 9 7
5 7 6 8 9 3 2 4 1
2 4 3 7 1 5 6 8 9
9 1 8 6 4 2 3 7 5
1 6 2 5 7 8 9 3 4
3 5 9 1 2 4 7 6 8
4 8 7 3 6 9 1 5 2
```

7
```
2 3 9 8 1 4 7 5 6
1 4 8 7 6 5 9 2 3
5 7 6 9 3 2 8 1 4
4 9 7 1 8 3 5 6 2
8 2 3 6 5 7 4 9 1
6 5 1 4 2 9 3 8 7
7 1 2 3 9 8 6 4 5
3 8 5 2 4 6 1 7 9
9 6 4 5 7 1 2 3 8
```

8
```
1 2 3 4 9 6 7 5 8
9 4 5 1 7 8 2 6 3
8 6 7 2 3 5 4 1 9
6 9 4 3 1 2 5 8 7
2 3 8 6 5 7 1 9 4
5 7 1 9 8 4 3 2 6
7 5 2 8 4 9 6 3 1
3 8 6 7 2 1 9 4 5
4 1 9 5 6 3 8 7 2
```

9
```
5 3 4 7 8 2 1 6 9
9 7 2 1 6 3 5 8 4
1 6 8 5 9 4 2 7 3
4 1 5 6 2 7 3 9 8
8 2 7 3 1 9 4 5 6
6 9 3 4 5 8 7 2 1
7 4 6 9 3 5 8 1 2
3 8 9 2 7 1 6 4 5
2 5 1 8 4 6 9 3 7
```

10
```
4 2 9 8 1 7 6 5 3
8 7 5 6 2 3 4 9 1
3 6 1 4 5 9 8 7 2
1 8 3 7 6 2 9 4 5
6 5 7 9 4 1 3 2 8
9 4 2 3 8 5 7 1 6
7 1 4 2 3 6 5 8 9
2 9 6 5 7 8 1 3 4
5 3 8 1 9 4 2 6 7
```

11
```
8 9 5 3 2 7 1 4 6
6 2 7 4 8 1 5 9 3
1 4 3 6 5 9 7 8 2
7 3 1 9 6 2 4 5 8
9 5 2 8 4 3 6 7 1
4 8 6 1 7 5 2 3 9
3 7 8 5 1 6 9 2 4
5 6 9 2 3 4 8 1 7
2 1 4 7 9 8 3 6 5
```

12
```
2 7 9 8 1 6 5 4 3
5 8 6 2 3 4 1 9 7
3 4 1 7 5 9 6 2 8
6 9 4 3 2 8 7 1 5
8 3 5 9 7 1 4 6 2
1 2 7 6 4 5 3 8 9
7 1 8 4 9 3 2 5 6
4 6 2 5 8 7 9 3 1
9 5 3 1 6 2 8 7 4
```

13
```
2 7 9 1 4 5 3 8 6
1 5 8 3 6 7 4 9 2
3 4 6 9 8 2 7 5 1
5 2 3 8 7 9 1 6 4
7 9 1 6 2 4 5 3 8
8 6 4 5 1 3 9 2 7
9 8 2 7 5 1 6 4 3
6 3 7 4 9 8 2 1 5
4 1 5 2 3 6 8 7 9
```

14
```
6 4 5 1 7 9 3 8 2
9 8 1 6 2 3 4 5 7
7 2 3 5 4 8 9 6 1
4 7 6 8 3 1 5 2 9
5 1 8 2 9 7 6 4 3
3 9 2 4 6 5 7 1 8
8 3 4 9 5 2 1 7 6
1 5 7 3 8 6 2 9 4
2 6 9 7 1 4 8 3 5
```

15
```
9 5 3 6 1 8 4 7 2
6 8 2 4 9 7 5 3 1
7 4 1 3 5 2 8 9 6
2 6 4 7 3 9 1 8 5
3 1 8 5 2 4 7 6 9
5 7 9 8 6 1 3 2 4
1 3 5 9 7 6 2 4 8
8 2 6 1 4 3 9 5 7
4 9 7 2 8 5 6 1 3
```

16
```
7 2 6 8 5 4 9 1 3
5 4 1 3 2 9 6 7 8
8 9 3 6 7 1 4 2 5
9 3 8 5 4 2 7 6 1
2 7 5 9 1 6 3 8 4
6 1 4 7 8 3 5 9 2
3 5 2 1 6 7 8 4 9
4 6 9 2 3 8 1 5 7
1 8 7 4 9 5 2 3 6
```

17
```
9 7 8 4 3 6 5 1 2
5 2 4 8 7 1 6 9 3
3 1 6 2 5 9 4 8 7
1 6 5 9 4 7 2 3 8
8 9 7 3 2 5 1 4 6
2 4 3 6 1 8 7 5 9
7 5 9 1 6 3 8 2 4
4 3 1 7 8 2 9 6 5
6 8 2 5 9 4 3 7 1
```

18
```
5 8 3 9 7 1 4 6 2
9 1 2 6 8 4 7 3 5
6 7 4 3 5 2 9 1 8
7 3 5 2 4 8 1 9 6
4 6 1 7 9 5 8 2 3
8 2 9 1 3 6 5 4 7
1 4 8 5 2 3 6 7 9
2 9 6 8 1 7 3 5 4
3 5 7 4 6 9 2 8 1
```

19
```
9 5 1 7 3 4 6 2 8
7 8 3 1 6 2 9 4 5
6 2 4 8 5 9 3 1 7
4 1 6 5 7 3 8 9 2
2 3 9 6 4 8 7 5 1
8 7 5 9 2 1 4 3 6
1 9 2 3 8 6 5 7 4
3 6 7 4 1 5 2 8 9
5 4 8 2 9 7 1 6 3
```

20
```
4 5 1 9 8 7 6 2 3
2 9 3 4 1 6 5 7 8
8 7 6 2 5 3 9 4 1
7 2 9 3 6 5 1 8 4
1 8 4 7 2 9 3 6 5
3 6 5 1 4 8 2 9 7
5 1 2 8 9 4 7 3 6
6 4 7 5 3 2 8 1 9
9 3 8 6 7 1 4 5 2
```

21
```
7 5 4 2 9 3 1 8 6
2 6 9 1 7 8 3 4 5
8 1 3 6 4 5 9 2 7
9 3 1 4 5 6 8 7 2
4 8 7 3 1 2 6 5 9
6 2 5 9 8 7 4 3 1
5 4 8 7 6 1 2 9 3
3 7 6 8 2 9 5 1 4
1 9 2 5 3 4 7 6 8
```

22
```
8 6 2 7 3 9 1 5 4
3 5 7 6 4 1 8 2 9
1 9 4 8 2 5 3 6 7
4 8 6 3 5 7 9 1 2
2 3 1 9 6 8 4 7 5
9 7 5 4 1 2 6 3 8
6 4 3 2 8 6 5 9 1
6 1 9 7 5 4 2 8 3
5 2 8 1 9 3 7 4 6
```

23
```
8 6 3 7 1 2 4 5 9
4 9 2 6 8 5 1 3 7
5 7 1 3 9 4 8 2 6
9 5 8 4 3 7 2 6 1
1 4 6 9 2 8 5 7 3
3 2 7 1 5 6 9 4 8
6 8 5 2 7 1 3 9 4
2 3 4 8 6 9 7 1 5
7 1 9 5 4 3 6 8 2
```

24
```
1 4 9 7 5 6 3 8 2
6 5 2 4 8 3 1 7 9
8 3 7 1 2 9 5 4 6
7 9 5 8 3 4 2 6 1
2 1 6 5 9 7 4 3 8
3 8 4 6 1 2 7 9 5
9 6 3 2 7 5 8 1 4
4 2 8 3 6 1 9 5 7
5 7 1 9 4 8 6 2 3
```

25
```
2 9 7 1 6 3 8 5 4
5 1 3 9 8 4 2 6 7
4 6 8 7 5 2 9 3 1
3 5 2 8 9 7 1 4 6
1 4 9 2 3 6 7 8 5
8 7 6 5 4 1 3 2 9
6 2 1 4 7 8 5 9 3
9 8 4 3 1 5 6 7 2
7 3 5 6 2 9 4 1 8
```

26
```
2 3 6 9 4 1 7 5 8
4 9 5 8 7 6 2 1 3
7 1 8 5 2 3 4 6 9
9 4 3 2 8 5 1 7 6
8 6 7 3 1 4 5 9 2
5 2 9 7 3 8 6 4 1
6 8 1 4 5 2 9 3 7
3 7 4 1 6 9 8 2 5
```

27
```
6 8 1 5 4 9 7 3 2
3 7 4 6 2 8 1 5 9
5 9 2 7 1 3 4 8 6
8 6 3 4 9 5 2 7 1
7 1 5 8 6 2 9 4 3
1 3 4 6 7 2 8 9 5
1 5 8 2 3 4 6 9 7
9 3 6 1 8 7 5 2 4
2 4 7 9 5 6 3 1 8
```

28
```
3 7 1 5 2 6 4 9 8
2 5 8 1 4 9 7 6 3
4 9 6 3 8 7 1 2 5
6 4 3 7 5 1 9 8 2
9 1 2 8 6 3 5 7 4
5 8 7 2 9 4 3 1 6
1 3 4 6 7 2 8 5 9
8 2 9 4 1 5 6 3 7
7 6 5 9 3 8 2 4 1
```

29
```
5 7 3 9 1 4 2 6 8
2 1 8 7 6 3 9 5 4
6 4 9 2 5 8 7 3 1
7 8 4 6 9 2 5 1 3
3 9 5 4 8 1 6 7 2
1 2 6 3 7 5 8 4 9
9 3 2 5 4 7 1 8 6
4 5 1 8 2 6 3 9 7
8 6 7 1 3 9 4 2 5
```

30
```
4 6 8 7 1 5 3 2 9
3 2 9 4 8 6 5 1 7
1 7 5 2 3 9 6 4 8
9 8 2 5 4 1 7 3 6
6 1 7 9 2 3 4 8 5
5 3 4 8 6 7 2 9 1
8 5 6 3 9 4 1 7 2
7 9 3 1 5 2 8 6 4
2 4 1 6 7 8 9 5 3
```

31
```
5 2 4 1 7 8 3 9 6
9 7 3 2 6 4 5 8 1
6 8 1 5 9 3 4 2 7
2 9 5 3 4 1 6 7 8
4 6 7 8 2 9 1 5 3
1 3 8 6 5 7 2 4 9
3 4 6 7 8 5 9 1 2
8 1 9 4 3 2 7 6 5
7 5 2 9 1 6 8 3 4
```

32
```
6 9 2 5 1 3 4 7 8
1 5 4 8 6 7 3 9 2
3 8 7 9 4 2 6 5 1
2 4 1 7 9 6 8 3 5
8 3 5 1 2 4 7 6 9
7 6 9 3 5 8 1 2 4
5 1 3 6 8 9 2 4 7
4 7 8 2 3 5 9 1 6
9 2 6 4 7 1 5 8 3
```

33
```
4 3 1 2 6 8 7 5 9
9 8 2 5 1 7 4 3 6
5 6 7 4 9 3 2 1 8
6 7 3 8 5 1 9 2 4
1 5 4 6 2 9 3 8 7
2 9 8 7 3 4 5 6 1
3 2 9 1 4 6 8 7 5
7 4 6 3 8 5 1 9 2
8 1 5 9 7 2 6 4 3
```

34
```
2 9 3 7 4 1 6 5 8
5 4 8 2 3 6 1 7 9
6 7 1 8 9 5 2 3 4
7 8 2 9 6 3 5 4 1
1 6 4 5 7 2 8 9 3
9 3 5 4 1 8 7 6 2
4 1 9 6 2 7 3 8 5
3 5 7 1 8 9 4 2 6
8 2 6 3 5 4 9 1 7
```

35
```
2 6 3 8 9 7 5 4 1
5 7 4 1 6 2 9 8 3
9 1 8 4 3 5 2 7 6
3 2 7 9 5 8 1 6 4
8 9 6 7 1 4 3 2 5
1 4 5 3 2 6 8 9 7
6 8 1 2 4 3 7 5 9
7 5 9 6 8 1 4 3 2
4 3 2 5 7 9 6 1 8
```

36
```
6 3 2 9 8 1 5 7 4
7 5 1 2 6 4 8 3 9
9 8 4 7 5 3 2 1 6
1 6 8 5 3 7 4 9 2
2 7 3 4 9 8 6 5 1
5 4 9 6 1 2 7 8 3
3 2 7 1 4 5 9 6 8
8 9 5 3 2 6 1 4 7
4 1 6 8 7 9 3 2 5
```

37
```
6 4 3 7 1 2 9 8 5
8 7 9 3 6 5 2 4 1
5 2 1 4 8 9 3 6 7
4 9 2 8 3 7 5 1 6
7 5 6 1 2 4 8 9 3
1 3 8 5 9 6 4 7 2
3 8 4 6 5 1 7 2 9
2 6 5 9 7 8 1 3 4
9 1 7 2 4 3 6 5 8
```

38
```
5 3 6 7 4 1 8 9 2
8 1 7 3 9 2 6 4 5
9 4 2 5 6 8 1 7 3
4 5 8 2 1 6 9 3 7
6 7 9 4 5 3 2 1 8
3 2 1 8 7 9 5 6 4
7 6 3 1 8 5 4 2 9
2 9 5 6 3 4 7 8 1
1 8 4 9 2 7 3 5 6
```

39
```
4 9 1 5 2 6 8 7 3
3 7 6 9 1 8 5 2 4
2 5 8 3 4 7 6 9 1
9 6 2 8 5 1 4 3 7
5 1 7 4 9 3 2 6 8
8 4 3 7 6 2 9 1 5
6 8 4 1 7 9 3 5 2
1 3 9 2 8 5 7 4 6
7 2 5 6 3 4 1 8 9
```

40
```
9 5 6 4 2 7 8 1 3
8 1 7 9 3 6 4 2 5
3 2 4 5 8 1 7 9 6
2 4 8 6 5 3 9 7 1
5 3 1 7 4 9 2 6 8
7 6 9 8 1 2 3 5 4
6 8 3 2 9 5 1 4 7
1 9 5 3 7 4 6 8 2
4 7 2 1 6 8 5 3 9
```

41
```
4 8 1 9 5 6 3 7 2
9 7 5 2 1 3 4 6 8
6 2 3 4 7 8 1 5 9
2 6 4 5 3 1 8 9 7
3 1 7 8 9 2 5 4 6
5 9 8 6 4 7 2 1 3
7 3 2 1 6 4 9 8 5
8 4 9 7 2 5 6 3 1
1 5 6 3 8 9 7 2 4
```

42
```
3 6 7 8 2 9 1 4 5
1 8 2 3 4 5 6 7 9
5 9 4 7 1 6 8 3 2
8 4 6 5 7 1 2 9 3
9 1 5 6 3 2 4 8 7
7 2 3 4 9 8 5 6 1
4 5 1 9 6 3 7 2 8
2 7 9 1 8 4 3 5 6
6 3 8 2 5 7 9 1 4
```

43
```
4 3 2 8 6 7 1 9 5
7 9 6 5 4 1 8 2 3
8 1 5 2 3 9 6 7 4
5 8 9 4 2 6 7 3 1
6 7 4 3 1 8 2 5 9
1 2 3 7 9 5 4 8 6
9 5 8 6 7 4 3 1 2
3 4 7 1 5 2 9 6 8
2 6 1 9 8 3 5 4 7
```

44
```
3 7 4 5 2 8 1 6 9
8 9 6 3 4 1 2 7 5
2 1 5 6 7 9 8 3 4
5 4 3 8 1 6 7 9 2
6 2 1 4 9 7 3 5 8
7 8 9 2 5 3 4 1 6
1 3 2 9 6 4 5 8 7
9 5 8 7 3 2 6 4 1
4 6 7 1 8 5 9 2 3
```

45
```
6 1 7 4 3 8 2 5 9
8 5 2 1 6 9 3 4 7
9 3 4 7 2 5 8 6 1
3 2 5 6 9 7 1 8 4
4 8 9 5 1 3 6 7 2
1 7 6 2 8 4 9 3 5
5 9 1 3 7 6 4 2 8
2 4 3 8 5 1 7 9 6
7 6 8 9 4 2 5 1 3
```

46
```
4 1 6 8 3 2 5 7 9
5 3 2 7 9 1 4 6 8
7 8 9 5 6 4 3 1 2
9 2 7 6 4 3 1 8 5
3 4 8 1 5 7 9 2 6
1 6 5 9 2 8 7 3 4
8 9 3 2 1 5 6 4 7
6 7 4 3 8 9 2 5 1
2 5 1 4 7 6 8 9 3
```

47
```
8 9 2 4 1 7 3 5 6
1 5 7 2 6 3 9 4 8
4 3 6 8 5 9 7 2 1
3 2 4 5 7 6 8 1 9
5 8 9 3 2 1 4 6 7
6 7 1 9 8 4 5 3 2
2 4 5 6 9 8 1 7 3
9 1 3 7 4 2 6 8 5
7 6 8 1 3 5 2 9 4
```

48
```
8 2 9 3 7 6 4 1 5
6 3 5 4 8 1 9 2 7
1 7 4 5 9 2 3 8 6
4 1 8 9 2 7 6 5 3
3 9 6 8 1 5 7 4 2
7 5 2 6 4 3 1 9 8
9 6 3 2 5 4 8 7 1
2 4 1 7 3 8 5 6 9
5 8 7 1 6 9 2 3 4
```

49
```
4 2 6 8 3 5 1 7 9
3 8 7 9 2 1 5 4 6
5 9 1 4 7 6 3 2 8
1 4 2 5 8 7 6 9 3
9 7 8 3 6 4 2 5 1
6 5 3 2 1 9 4 8 7
7 3 4 1 5 8 9 6 2
8 1 5 6 9 2 7 3 4
2 6 9 7 4 3 8 1 5
```

50
```
5 2 4 8 9 6 7 3 1
3 1 9 4 7 2 8 5 6
8 7 6 1 5 3 2 9 4
1 9 2 6 8 7 3 4 5
4 6 8 3 2 5 9 1 7
7 5 3 9 4 1 6 8 2
6 3 5 2 1 8 4 7 9
2 4 1 7 3 9 5 6 8
9 8 7 5 6 4 1 2 3
```

51
```
6 3 2 5 9 1 8 7 4
7 1 4 2 8 6 3 9 5
8 5 9 7 3 4 2 6 1
4 7 5 6 2 8 1 3 9
9 2 8 1 7 3 5 4 6
3 6 1 4 5 9 7 8 2
2 4 3 9 1 7 6 5 8
5 9 7 8 6 2 4 1 3
1 8 6 3 4 5 9 2 7
```

52
```
8 9 7 6 4 2 3 1 5
6 2 3 5 8 1 7 9 4
1 4 5 7 3 9 8 6 2
3 5 9 4 2 8 6 7 1
7 8 4 3 1 6 5 2 9
2 1 6 9 5 7 4 3 8
4 7 1 2 6 5 9 8 3
5 6 8 1 9 3 2 4 7
9 3 2 8 7 4 1 5 6
```

53
```
7 2 9 4 3 1 5 6 8
3 4 8 2 6 5 7 9 1
1 5 6 8 9 7 3 2 4
9 8 7 5 4 2 1 3 6
4 6 5 7 1 3 9 8 2
2 1 3 9 8 6 4 5 7
6 3 2 1 5 4 8 7 9
8 7 4 3 2 9 6 1 5
5 9 1 6 7 8 2 4 3
```

54
```
8 9 7 3 1 6 4 2 5
3 2 1 7 4 5 8 9 6
6 5 4 2 9 8 3 1 7
2 4 3 5 7 1 6 8 9
5 1 6 8 2 9 7 4 3
7 8 9 6 3 4 1 5 2
1 7 8 9 5 3 2 6 4
4 3 5 1 6 2 9 7 8
9 6 2 4 8 7 5 3 1
```

55
```
7 5 4 1 9 8 6 3 2
2 1 9 7 3 6 4 8 5
6 3 8 4 2 5 1 9 7
5 6 3 9 8 2 7 4 1
8 2 1 5 7 4 3 6 9
4 9 7 3 6 1 5 2 8
9 8 5 6 4 7 2 1 3
1 4 2 8 5 3 9 7 6
3 7 6 2 1 9 8 5 4
```

56
```
2 5 8 7 4 6 3 1 9
6 7 3 1 2 9 8 5 4
4 1 9 8 3 5 6 7 2
1 3 5 4 9 8 7 2 6
8 6 7 2 5 1 4 9 3
9 4 2 6 7 3 1 8 5
3 8 1 9 6 2 5 4 7
5 2 4 3 8 7 9 6 1
7 9 6 5 1 4 2 3 8
```

57
```
7 1 6 5 3 4 8 9 2
4 8 9 2 6 1 7 5 3
3 5 2 7 9 8 1 6 4
1 6 4 9 5 7 3 2 8
9 3 8 6 1 2 4 7 5
5 2 7 8 4 3 6 1 9
6 7 5 4 8 9 2 3 1
2 4 3 1 7 5 9 8 6
8 9 1 3 2 6 5 4 7
```

58
```
9 6 2 7 5 4 1 3 8
7 8 4 1 3 9 6 5 2
3 1 5 2 8 6 7 4 9
2 7 3 4 6 5 9 8 1
4 9 8 3 1 2 5 6 7
6 5 1 8 9 7 4 2 3
8 3 6 5 7 1 2 9 4
5 4 7 9 2 8 3 1 6
1 2 9 6 4 3 8 7 5
```

59
```
2 3 7 6 1 5 9 4 8
9 5 4 8 3 2 1 7 6
1 8 6 7 9 4 5 2 3
5 6 9 1 4 7 3 8 2
7 1 2 3 8 6 4 9 5
3 4 8 5 2 9 7 6 1
4 9 1 2 6 3 8 5 7
6 7 3 9 5 8 2 1 4
8 2 5 4 7 1 6 3 9
```

60
```
4 1 2 6 9 8 3 5 7
7 6 9 4 5 3 2 8 1
3 8 5 1 7 2 4 6 9
8 2 1 9 6 7 5 3 4
5 7 6 3 1 4 8 9 2
9 3 4 2 8 5 7 1 6
1 5 8 7 4 6 9 2 3
6 4 3 5 2 9 1 7 8
2 9 7 8 3 1 6 4 5
```

61
```
4 5 1 2 8 6 7 9 3
7 6 2 5 9 3 1 4 8
9 3 8 1 4 7 5 2 6
2 7 3 9 6 4 8 5 1
5 8 6 7 1 2 9 3 4
1 9 4 8 3 5 2 6 7
8 4 7 3 5 9 6 1 2
6 1 9 4 2 8 3 7 5
3 2 5 6 7 1 4 8 9
```

62
```
2 9 6 3 5 8 4 7 1
5 8 4 1 6 7 2 9 3
7 3 1 2 4 9 8 6 5
6 2 3 7 1 5 9 8 4
4 1 9 8 3 6 5 2 7
8 5 7 4 9 2 3 1 6
3 4 8 9 7 1 6 5 2
1 6 2 5 8 4 7 3 9
9 7 5 6 2 3 1 4 8
```

63
```
6 1 3 2 5 9 7 8 4
8 5 9 7 4 6 1 3 2
7 2 4 8 3 1 5 9 6
1 4 7 5 6 8 3 2 9
3 9 2 4 1 7 6 5 8
5 6 8 3 9 2 4 1 7
2 8 5 6 7 3 9 4 1
4 7 1 9 8 5 2 6 3
9 3 6 1 2 4 8 7 5
```

64
```
2 1 5 9 4 8 6 7 3
4 3 9 1 7 6 2 5 8
7 6 8 2 5 3 1 9 4
9 4 2 5 8 7 3 1 6
1 5 6 3 9 4 7 8 2
8 7 3 6 1 2 9 4 5
6 9 7 4 2 5 8 3 1
5 2 1 8 3 9 4 6 7
3 8 4 7 6 1 5 2 9
```

65
```
4 5 9 2 8 3 1 7 6
6 8 7 4 1 9 3 5 2
1 2 3 5 7 6 9 4 8
5 7 2 3 9 4 8 6 1
9 6 4 8 2 1 5 3 7
3 1 8 6 5 7 4 2 9
7 3 5 9 6 8 2 1 4
2 9 1 7 4 5 6 8 3
8 4 6 1 3 2 7 9 5
```

66
```
9 5 2 1 3 4 8 6 7
6 8 4 7 9 2 5 3 1
1 3 7 5 6 8 4 9 2
7 6 8 2 5 1 3 4 9
5 1 9 6 4 3 7 2 8
2 4 3 8 7 9 6 1 5
8 2 5 4 1 6 9 7 3
3 7 6 9 2 5 1 8 4
4 9 1 3 8 7 2 5 6
```

67
```
1 9 4 8 6 3 5 2 7
6 8 7 5 4 2 3 9 1
2 5 3 1 9 7 8 6 4
9 4 2 7 5 6 1 3 8
5 3 1 4 2 8 6 7 9
7 6 8 3 1 9 4 5 2
8 2 6 9 3 1 7 4 5
3 7 5 2 8 4 9 1 6
4 1 9 6 7 5 2 8 3
```

68
```
9 2 6 7 3 8 4 1 5
5 4 7 9 2 1 3 6 8
1 3 8 5 6 4 9 7 2
3 7 1 6 5 9 2 8 4
6 5 4 2 8 3 1 9 7
2 8 9 1 4 7 6 5 3
7 9 5 4 1 2 8 3 6
8 6 2 3 9 5 7 4 1
4 1 3 8 7 6 5 2 9
```

69
```
3 8 1 2 7 9 5 6 4
9 4 6 1 5 3 8 2 7
5 2 7 4 8 6 9 3 1
8 5 2 3 1 4 6 7 9
1 7 4 9 6 8 3 5 2
6 3 9 7 2 5 1 4 8
7 1 8 5 3 2 4 9 6
2 9 5 6 4 1 7 8 3
4 6 3 8 9 7 2 1 5
```

70
```
2 4 3 7 5 6 9 1 8
7 9 1 4 8 2 5 3 6
5 6 8 9 3 1 7 4 2
6 5 2 1 9 3 8 7 4
1 8 7 5 2 4 6 9 3
9 3 4 8 6 7 1 2 5
8 1 9 2 4 5 3 6 7
3 2 5 6 7 9 4 8 1
4 7 6 3 1 8 2 5 9
```

71
```
8 5 6 4 7 9 1 2 3
1 4 7 3 8 2 5 6 9
2 9 3 6 1 5 7 4 8
3 2 4 9 5 6 8 1 7
7 8 5 1 2 3 4 9 6
6 1 9 7 4 8 2 3 5
9 7 2 8 6 1 3 5 4
5 3 8 2 9 4 6 7 1
4 6 1 5 3 7 9 8 2
```

72
```
8 4 7 5 1 3 2 9 6
9 6 1 4 8 2 7 5 3
3 5 2 7 9 6 4 1 8
6 2 3 1 5 7 9 8 4
4 7 8 6 3 9 5 2 1
1 9 5 2 4 8 3 6 7
7 8 4 9 6 5 1 3 2
2 3 9 8 7 1 6 4 5
5 1 6 3 2 4 8 7 9
```

73
```
1 6 7 9 3 4 2 8 5
9 4 2 5 8 1 7 6 3
3 8 5 6 7 2 9 4 1
7 2 1 8 6 3 5 9 4
5 3 4 1 9 7 6 2 8
8 9 6 2 4 5 1 3 7
2 5 3 4 1 6 8 7 9
6 7 8 3 5 9 4 1 2
4 1 9 7 2 8 3 5 6
```

74
```
6 4 1 2 5 3 7 9 8
7 9 8 6 1 4 5 3 2
3 2 5 7 9 8 4 1 6
1 8 6 4 3 7 2 5 9
9 5 3 1 8 2 6 4 7
4 7 2 9 6 5 1 8 3
5 6 9 3 7 1 8 2 4
8 3 4 5 2 6 9 7 1
2 1 7 8 4 9 3 6 5
```

75
```
6 8 1 5 3 2 4 7 9
5 3 4 7 8 9 2 1 6
2 7 9 4 6 1 5 3 8
9 2 3 1 4 7 6 8 5
7 1 5 8 2 6 9 4 3
8 4 6 9 5 3 7 2 1
1 5 8 6 7 4 3 9 2
4 9 2 3 1 5 8 6 7
3 6 7 2 9 8 1 5 4
```

76
```
6 4 5 7 3 2 9 1 8
8 3 9 5 4 1 6 2 7
1 7 2 6 8 9 3 4 5
5 1 8 3 7 6 4 9 2
7 9 3 2 1 4 5 8 6
2 6 4 8 9 5 1 7 3
3 2 1 4 6 8 7 5 9
9 8 7 1 5 3 2 6 4
4 5 6 9 2 7 8 3 1
```

77
```
5 3 1 7 2 9 4 8 6
8 6 9 5 3 4 2 7 1
4 7 2 1 6 8 9 5 3
3 1 4 8 5 2 7 6 9
9 5 6 4 1 7 8 3 2
7 2 8 3 9 6 1 4 5
1 8 3 9 7 5 6 2 4
6 9 7 2 4 3 5 1 8
2 4 5 6 8 1 3 9 7
```

78
```
7 5 8 1 3 9 2 6 4
9 2 6 4 5 8 3 1 7
3 4 1 7 2 6 8 5 9
6 9 5 3 4 2 1 7 8
4 8 3 6 7 1 9 2 5
2 1 7 9 8 5 6 4 3
1 3 9 5 6 4 7 8 2
8 7 4 2 1 3 5 9 6
5 6 2 8 9 7 4 3 1
```

79
```
3 1 6 8 4 2 9 5 7
8 2 9 5 1 7 4 6 3
4 5 7 6 3 9 1 2 8
2 7 4 1 5 8 3 9 6
9 6 5 3 2 4 8 7 1
1 8 3 7 9 6 2 4 5
5 9 8 4 7 1 6 3 2
7 4 1 2 6 3 5 8 9
6 3 2 9 8 5 7 1 4
```

80
```
7 6 3 9 4 1 2 5 8
9 2 5 8 6 3 4 1 7
1 4 8 2 7 5 3 6 9
2 8 4 1 3 6 7 9 5
5 1 9 7 2 8 6 4 3
6 3 7 4 5 9 8 2 1
3 7 6 5 1 4 9 8 2
8 5 2 6 9 7 1 3 4
4 9 1 3 8 2 5 7 6
```

81
```
6 7 1 2 9 3 8 4 5
2 8 5 1 6 4 3 9 7
9 3 4 7 8 5 2 6 1
4 5 9 3 1 2 7 8 6
7 6 8 5 4 9 1 2 3
3 1 2 8 7 6 4 5 9
1 4 6 9 3 8 5 7 2
5 9 7 4 2 1 6 3 8
8 2 3 6 5 7 9 1 4
```

82
```
4 3 9 7 1 5 6 8 2
2 7 6 8 3 4 9 5 1
8 1 5 2 9 6 4 7 3
3 5 2 6 4 8 1 9 7
7 9 8 1 5 3 2 6 4
1 6 4 9 7 2 8 3 5
5 4 1 3 6 9 7 2 8
6 2 7 5 8 1 3 4 9
9 8 3 4 2 7 5 1 6
```

83
```
4 6 9 1 7 3 8 2 5
7 3 2 8 9 5 4 6 1
5 8 1 6 4 2 3 7 9
6 1 4 2 5 7 9 8 3
3 9 8 4 1 6 2 5 7
2 5 7 9 3 8 6 1 4
1 2 3 5 8 4 7 9 6
8 4 5 7 6 9 1 3 2
9 7 6 3 2 1 5 4 8
```

84
```
7 8 4 3 1 6 9 2 5
6 3 1 2 5 9 7 8 4
5 2 9 7 8 4 6 1 3
1 5 6 8 9 2 3 4 7
3 7 8 4 6 1 2 5 9
9 4 2 5 3 7 8 6 1
8 1 3 6 7 5 4 9 2
2 6 5 9 4 3 1 7 8
4 9 7 1 2 8 5 3 6
```

85
```
3 8 1 2 7 9 5 6 4
9 4 6 1 5 3 8 2 7
5 2 7 4 8 6 9 3 1
8 5 2 3 1 4 6 7 9
1 7 4 9 6 8 3 5 2
6 3 9 7 2 5 1 4 8
7 1 8 5 3 2 4 9 6
2 9 5 6 4 1 7 8 3
4 6 3 8 9 7 2 1 5
```

86
```
2 4 3 7 5 6 9 1 8
7 9 1 4 8 2 5 3 6
5 6 8 9 3 1 7 4 2
6 5 2 1 9 3 8 7 4
1 8 7 5 2 4 6 9 3
9 3 4 8 6 7 1 2 5
8 1 9 2 4 5 3 6 7
3 2 5 6 7 9 4 8 1
4 7 6 3 1 8 2 5 9
```

87
```
8 5 6 4 7 9 1 2 3
1 4 7 3 8 2 5 6 9
2 9 3 6 1 5 7 4 8
3 2 4 9 5 6 8 1 7
7 8 5 1 2 3 4 9 6
6 1 9 7 4 8 2 3 5
9 7 2 8 6 1 3 5 4
5 3 8 2 9 4 6 7 1
4 6 1 5 3 7 9 8 2
```

88
```
8 4 7 5 1 3 2 9 6
9 6 1 4 8 2 7 5 3
3 5 2 7 9 6 4 1 8
6 2 3 1 5 7 9 8 4
4 7 8 6 3 9 5 2 1
1 9 5 2 4 8 3 6 7
7 8 4 9 6 5 1 3 2
2 3 9 8 7 1 6 4 5
5 1 6 3 2 4 8 7 9
```

89
```
1 6 7 9 3 4 2 8 5
9 4 2 5 8 1 7 6 3
3 8 5 6 7 2 9 4 1
7 2 1 8 6 3 5 9 4
5 3 4 1 9 7 6 2 8
8 9 6 2 4 5 1 3 7
2 5 3 4 1 6 8 7 9
6 7 8 3 5 9 4 1 2
4 1 9 7 2 8 3 5 6
```

90
```
6 4 1 2 5 3 7 9 8
7 9 8 6 1 4 5 3 2
3 2 5 7 9 8 4 1 6
1 8 6 4 3 7 2 5 9
9 5 3 1 8 2 6 4 7
4 7 2 9 6 5 1 8 3
5 6 9 3 7 1 8 2 4
8 3 4 5 2 6 9 7 1
2 1 7 8 4 9 3 6 5
```

91

6	8	1	5	3	2	4	7	9
5	3	4	7	8	9	2	1	6
2	7	9	4	6	1	5	3	8
9	2	3	1	4	7	6	8	5
7	1	5	8	2	6	9	4	3
8	4	6	9	5	3	7	2	1
1	5	8	6	7	4	3	9	2
4	9	2	3	1	5	8	6	7
3	6	7	2	9	8	1	5	4

92

6	4	5	7	3	2	9	1	8
8	3	9	5	4	1	6	2	7
1	7	2	6	8	9	3	4	5
5	1	8	3	7	6	4	9	2
7	9	3	2	1	4	5	8	6
2	6	4	8	9	5	1	7	3
3	2	1	4	6	8	7	5	9
9	8	7	1	5	3	2	6	4
4	5	6	9	2	7	8	3	1

93

4	9	2	6	7	8	3	1	5
1	6	7	3	4	5	8	2	9
8	5	3	2	1	9	6	4	7
5	3	4	8	2	7	1	9	6
6	2	9	1	3	4	5	7	8
7	8	1	5	9	6	2	3	4
3	7	8	4	6	1	9	5	2
2	4	6	9	5	3	7	8	1
9	1	5	7	8	2	4	6	3

94

3	1	4	6	8	9	7	2	5
7	8	9	2	4	5	3	6	1
6	5	2	7	1	3	9	8	4
9	6	7	5	3	8	4	1	2
4	3	8	1	9	2	6	5	7
5	2	1	4	6	7	8	9	3
1	7	6	9	2	4	5	3	8
2	4	3	8	5	6	1	7	9
8	9	5	3	7	1	2	4	6

95

3	1	5	6	7	2	4	8	9
6	9	2	8	4	3	1	5	7
7	4	8	1	9	5	6	2	3
2	6	4	3	8	1	7	9	5
8	7	9	4	5	6	3	1	2
1	5	3	7	2	9	8	6	4
4	2	7	9	6	8	5	3	1
9	8	1	5	3	7	2	4	6
5	3	6	2	1	4	9	7	8

96

4	2	1	9	5	3	6	8	7
7	5	6	1	8	4	3	9	2
3	8	9	6	2	7	4	1	5
8	6	5	2	4	9	1	7	3
2	1	4	7	3	8	9	5	6
9	7	3	5	6	1	8	2	4
6	3	2	8	9	5	7	4	1
5	9	7	4	1	6	2	3	8
1	4	8	3	7	2	5	6	9

97

2	4	9	1	7	3	5	8	6
3	5	7	8	4	6	1	9	2
8	1	6	5	9	2	7	4	3
1	7	2	9	6	8	4	3	5
4	6	8	3	5	1	2	7	9
5	9	3	4	2	7	8	6	1
9	2	4	7	3	5	6	1	8
6	3	1	2	8	4	9	5	7
7	8	5	6	1	9	3	2	4

98

5	3	2	8	4	1	6	7	9
1	9	6	5	3	7	2	8	4
4	7	8	9	6	2	5	3	1
7	4	1	3	2	5	8	9	6
3	6	9	4	1	8	7	2	5
2	8	5	6	7	9	1	4	3
6	1	7	2	9	4	3	5	8
9	5	3	7	8	6	4	1	2
8	2	4	1	5	3	9	6	7

99

1	4	9	2	8	6	7	3	5
7	6	5	1	9	3	2	4	8
3	8	2	5	7	4	6	9	1
5	2	4	9	1	7	3	8	6
9	3	6	4	2	8	5	1	7
8	7	1	3	6	5	4	2	9
4	1	8	7	5	2	9	6	3
2	9	7	6	3	1	8	5	4
6	5	3	8	4	9	1	7	2

100

3	9	1	8	4	2	5	6	7
2	5	7	9	6	1	4	8	3
6	4	8	7	3	5	9	1	2
7	6	2	4	8	9	1	3	5
9	8	5	6	1	3	2	7	4
4	1	3	2	5	7	6	9	8
8	3	4	5	9	6	7	2	1
1	7	6	3	2	4	8	5	9
5	2	9	1	7	8	3	4	6

101

9	2	3	4	5	8	1	6	7
8	1	7	3	6	9	5	4	2
6	5	4	1	2	7	9	8	3
3	6	1	8	7	2	4	5	9
2	4	5	9	1	6	3	7	8
7	8	9	5	4	3	2	1	6
5	3	2	6	8	1	7	9	4
4	7	8	2	9	5	6	3	1
1	9	6	7	3	4	8	2	5

102

3	9	1	2	6	8	4	5	7
8	6	7	3	5	4	1	2	9
4	2	5	9	7	1	3	6	8
9	1	6	8	4	5	7	3	2
2	7	3	6	1	9	8	4	5
5	8	4	7	2	3	6	9	1
7	3	9	4	8	2	5	1	6
1	4	8	5	9	6	2	7	3
6	5	2	1	3	7	9	8	4

103

3	1	5	8	7	6	4	9	2
9	7	4	5	2	1	8	3	6
2	8	6	9	4	3	1	5	7
1	3	8	2	6	5	9	7	4
5	2	9	7	3	4	6	1	8
6	4	7	1	9	8	5	2	3
8	9	3	6	1	7	2	4	5
7	6	1	4	5	2	3	8	9
4	5	2	3	8	9	7	6	1

104

3	7	5	4	2	1	8	6	9
2	1	6	7	8	9	3	4	5
9	8	4	6	3	5	1	2	7
8	5	2	3	4	7	9	1	6
6	9	7	2	1	8	4	5	3
1	4	3	5	9	6	7	8	2
4	3	1	9	6	2	5	7	8
5	6	9	8	7	4	2	3	1
7	2	8	1	5	3	6	9	4

105

1	9	3	7	6	8	2	5	4
6	8	7	4	5	2	9	1	3
2	4	5	1	3	9	6	7	8
8	3	4	9	1	6	7	2	5
5	7	1	8	2	3	4	9	6
9	2	6	5	4	7	8	3	1
3	6	8	2	9	5	1	4	7
4	5	2	6	7	1	3	8	9
7	1	9	3	8	4	5	6	2

106

2	3	7	1	5	4	9	8	6
1	9	8	7	6	3	5	2	4
5	4	6	2	9	8	3	1	7
8	1	9	4	3	7	6	5	2
7	6	2	9	1	5	4	3	8
4	5	3	6	8	2	7	9	1
9	7	1	3	2	6	8	4	5
6	2	5	8	4	9	1	7	3
3	8	4	5	7	1	2	6	9

107

5	9	3	6	4	7	8	1	2
4	7	6	2	8	1	5	3	9
8	1	2	9	5	3	6	4	7
9	3	7	4	2	6	1	8	5
2	6	8	3	1	5	9	7	4
1	4	5	8	7	9	2	6	3
6	5	1	7	9	4	3	2	8
7	2	9	1	3	8	4	5	6
3	8	4	5	6	2	7	9	1

108

6	1	7	2	5	8	3	4	9
3	8	5	6	9	4	1	7	2
4	2	9	7	1	3	6	8	5
1	3	2	4	8	9	7	5	6
7	4	6	3	2	5	9	1	8
5	9	8	1	7	6	4	2	3
2	5	4	9	6	1	8	3	7
9	7	3	8	4	2	5	6	1
8	6	1	5	3	7	2	9	4

109

2	4	9	7	1	8	6	5	3
6	1	7	3	9	5	8	2	4
3	8	5	2	4	6	1	9	7
1	3	6	5	2	7	9	4	8
8	9	2	6	3	4	7	1	5
5	7	4	1	8	9	2	3	6
4	2	1	8	7	3	5	6	9
7	6	3	9	5	2	4	8	1
9	5	8	4	6	1	3	7	2

110

4	6	5	1	9	3	7	2	8
8	1	2	7	6	4	3	9	5
7	3	9	8	5	2	4	6	1
5	2	6	3	4	7	1	8	9
9	7	8	6	1	5	2	4	3
3	4	1	2	8	9	6	5	7
6	5	4	9	7	1	8	3	2
1	9	3	4	2	8	5	7	6
2	8	7	5	3	6	9	1	4

111

6	3	7	9	8	5	1	4	2
9	2	1	6	3	4	5	8	7
8	4	5	7	1	2	3	9	6
2	7	8	3	9	6	4	1	5
3	5	4	1	2	7	8	6	9
1	6	9	4	5	8	2	7	3
5	9	2	8	7	1	6	3	4
4	8	3	5	6	9	7	2	1
7	1	6	2	4	3	9	5	8

112

1	6	8	4	5	3	2	7	9
5	9	3	8	7	2	6	4	1
4	7	2	6	9	1	5	8	3
9	3	1	5	6	7	4	2	8
2	8	7	1	3	4	9	6	5
6	5	4	2	8	9	3	1	7
7	1	6	9	2	5	8	3	4
3	2	5	7	4	8	1	9	6
8	4	9	3	1	6	7	5	2

113

9	8	2	7	6	5	1	4	3
7	4	5	1	3	9	6	8	2
1	6	3	4	8	2	7	5	9
6	9	8	2	1	4	5	3	7
4	2	7	3	5	6	8	9	1
5	3	1	9	7	8	4	2	6
3	5	9	6	4	1	2	7	8
8	7	6	5	2	3	9	1	4
2	1	4	8	9	7	3	6	5

114

9	4	7	6	5	3	1	8	2
6	3	8	7	1	2	4	5	9
2	1	5	4	9	8	3	7	6
7	9	3	1	4	6	8	2	5
5	2	6	8	3	7	9	4	1
4	8	1	5	2	9	6	3	7
1	7	9	3	8	5	2	6	4
8	6	4	2	7	1	5	9	3
3	5	2	9	6	4	7	1	8

115

4	1	5	3	8	9	2	6	7
6	9	8	2	4	7	1	5	3
3	7	2	6	5	1	9	4	8
7	4	9	8	3	6	5	1	2
2	6	3	4	1	5	7	8	9
8	5	1	7	9	2	4	3	6
9	3	6	1	7	4	8	2	5
5	8	4	9	2	3	6	7	1
1	2	7	5	6	8	3	9	4

116

7	1	6	9	3	4	2	8	5
9	5	4	2	8	1	3	7	6
3	8	2	6	7	5	4	1	9
8	6	1	7	2	9	5	4	3
5	2	9	4	1	3	8	6	7
4	3	7	5	6	8	1	9	2
1	9	3	8	5	7	6	2	4
6	4	8	3	9	2	7	5	1
2	7	5	1	4	6	9	3	8

117

1	7	9	8	6	3	5	4	2
6	5	4	7	2	9	1	8	3
2	8	3	1	5	4	9	6	7
3	6	2	4	8	5	7	9	1
7	9	8	2	1	6	4	3	5
5	4	1	3	9	7	6	2	8
4	3	5	9	7	8	2	1	6
8	1	6	5	4	2	3	7	9
9	2	7	6	3	1	8	5	4

118

9	2	3	4	5	8	7	6	1
4	6	1	3	2	7	8	5	9
8	5	7	6	1	9	4	2	3
3	9	2	7	8	5	6	1	4
7	1	6	9	4	3	2	8	5
5	8	4	1	6	2	3	9	7
2	3	9	5	7	6	1	4	8
6	4	5	8	3	1	9	7	2
1	7	8	2	9	4	5	3	6

Domino Chains pages 162-164

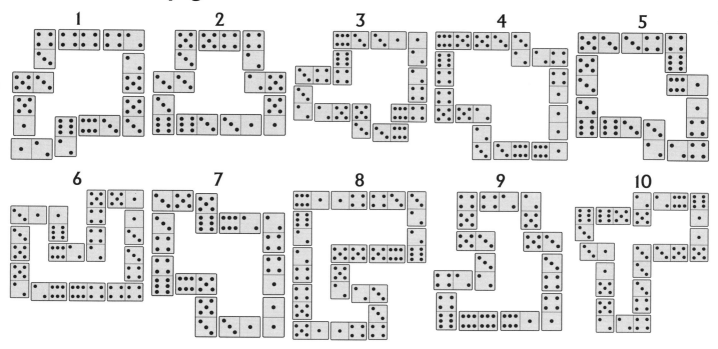

Number Searches pages 165-167

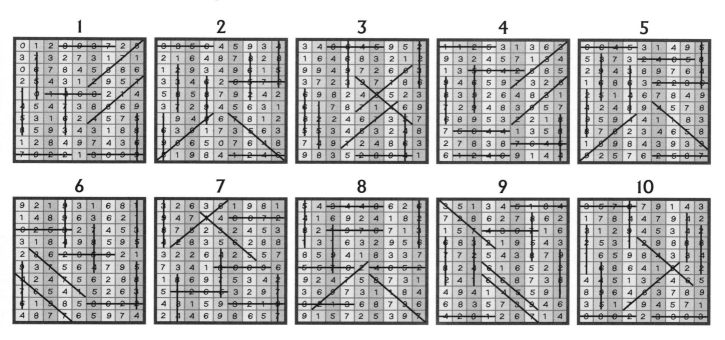

Tai-Chi Towers pages 192-193

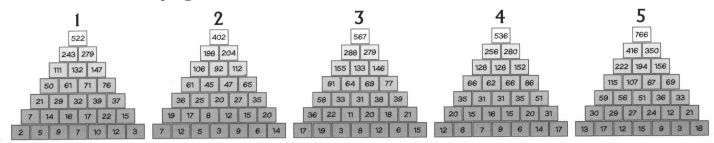

1

	522				
	243	279			
	111	132	147		
50	61	71	76		
21	29	32	39	37	
7	14	16	17	22	15
2	5	9	7	10	12	3

2

	402				
	198	204			
	106	92	112		
61	45	47	65		
36	25	20	27	35	
19	17	8	12	15	20
7	12	5	3	9	6	14

3

	567				
	288	279			
	155	133	146		
91	64	69	77		
58	33	31	38	39	
36	22	11	20	18	21
17	19	3	8	12	6	15

4

	536				
	256	280			
	128	128	152		
66	62	66	86		
35	31	31	35	51	
20	15	16	15	20	31
12	8	7	9	6	14	17

5

	766				
	416	350			
	222	194	156		
115	107	87	69		
59	56	51	36	33	
30	29	27	24	12	21
13	17	12	15	9	3	18

6

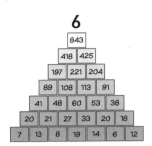

	843				
	418	425			
	197	221	204		
89	108	113	91		
41	48	60	53	38	
20	21	27	33	20	18
7	13	8	19	14	6	12

Cosmic Connectors pages 226-228

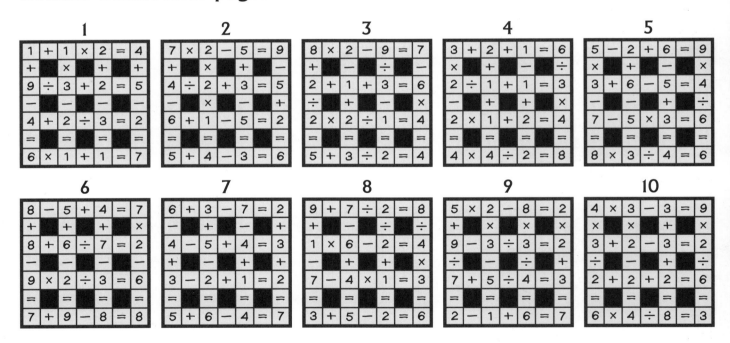

1

1	+	1	×	2	=	4
+		×		+		+
9	÷	3	+	2	=	5
−		−		−		−
4	+	2	÷	3	=	2
=		=		=		=
6	×	1	+	1	=	7

2

7	×	2	−	5	=	9
+		×		+		−
4	÷	2	+	3	=	5
−		×		−		+
6	+	1	−	5	=	2
=		=		=		=
5	+	4	−	3	=	6

3

8	×	2	−	9	=	7
+		−		÷		−
2	+	1	+	3	=	6
÷		+		−		×
2	×	2	÷	1	=	4
=		=		=		=
5	+	3	÷	2	=	4

4

3	+	2	+	1	=	6
×		+		−		÷
2	÷	1	+	1	=	3
−		+		+		×
2	×	1	+	2	=	4
=		=		=		=
4	×	4	÷	2	=	8

5

5	−	2	+	6	=	9
×		+		−		×
3	+	6	−	5	=	4
−		−		+		÷
7	−	5	×	3	=	6
=		=		=		=
8	×	3	÷	4	=	6

6

8	−	5	+	4	=	7
+		+		+		×
8	+	6	÷	7	=	2
−		−		−		−
9	×	2	÷	3	=	6
=		=		=		=
7	+	9	−	8	=	8

7

6	+	3	−	7	=	2
−		+		−		+
4	−	5	+	4	=	3
+		−		+		+
3	−	2	+	1	=	2
=		=		=		=
5	+	6	−	4	=	7

8

9	+	7	÷	2	=	8
+		−		÷		÷
1	×	6	−	2	=	4
−		+		+		×
7	−	4	×	1	=	3
=		=		=		=
3	+	5	−	2	=	6

9

5	×	2	−	8	=	2
+		×		×		×
9	−	3	÷	3	=	2
÷		−		÷		+
7	+	5	÷	4	=	3
=		=		=		=
2	−	1	+	6	=	7

10

4	×	3	−	3	=	9
×		×		+		×
3	+	2	−	3	=	2
÷		−		+		÷
2	+	2	+	2	=	6
=		=		=		=
6	×	4	÷	8	=	3